Your Guide to Mastering the
Vape Space

Published by Vape Publications

Costa Mesa, CA 92627

Copyright © 2014

No part of this book may be reproduced, stored in a retrieval system or transmitted by any means, electronic, mechanical, photocopying, recording or otherwise, without the written permission of the author.

For larger quantity sales, media interviews or speaking requests, contact service@VapeMentors.com

Written and printed in the United States of America

First edition October, 2014

ISBN-13:

978-1502823687

ISBN-10:

1502823683

Acknowledgements

As a famous rock song called "Truckin'" by the Grateful Dead (look it up if you're younger than 40...) once stated "What a long strange trip it's been," and indeed it has been an interesting ride. Check it out:
https://www.youtube.com/watch?v=pafY6sZt0FE

We often wonder if our lives can change with a singular event and I can assure you it can and it has. On July 4, 2013 I walked by a storefront in Newport Beach, California on my way to see the craziness at the beach during the wildest day of the year. I walked by this shop, stopped in my tracks and went inside and asked "**What the hell is a Vape Shop?**" What is a "Vape," why had I never heard of it before? After a brief conversation and an explanation of vaping and a feeling of déjà vu as I felt like I had transported back to 1977 to a head shop with all the colorful vials and pipes and weird things I could not identify, I said "That is awesome!" They told me that this was a way for people to quit smoking gradually and slowly dial back their tobacco addiction and nicotine delivery. Though I was never a smoker my mother was and I have known many over the years.

One conversation led to another, which led to lots and lots of research and many more questions than answers.

Where did this business come from? How many shops were there in Orange County where I lived? In California? In the country? Who typically opens a store like this? Some questions had answers, but most did not. I also discovered that this Vaping *Thing* was primarily led by a generation which I knew a lot about: Millennials, AKA, Generation Y. Two years prior I wrote a book called "Success Overnight: The Baby Boomer's and Gen Y Guide to becoming an

Overnight Success" which dissected the three predominant generations in society today:

- The Millennials
- Generation X (or Gen X)
- And Baby Boomers

As I researched and wrote my earlier book I developed a huge amount of respect for this Millennial Generation! They were brilliant. Socially conscious, adept at technology and social media, with generally giving and charitable spirits- they were born to be entrepreneurs. They had no false illusion of getting a job and retiring there 40 years later. They were risk takers. They could start a business in their dorms and a few years later sell it for millions of dollars. They had so much going for them and I was jealous! But I had some things that they lacked: experience. Patience. People skills. Put our two generations together and you have a powerful combination.

One of the things that has been very personal to me as I dealt with the financial devastation and aftermath from the recession which began in 2008 was the strong desire and urgency to "pass it on." Pass on my knowledge, my experience, the pain that I lived through and the failures that preceded them. I wanted this young, brilliant generation to avoid that trap and learn and that takes the form of **Mentorship**.

VapeMentors consults, but that is what we do, not who we are. There is a difference between guiding someone along in a strictly business to business transaction and mentorship, and though we do both, mentorship is our mission. Our clients learn from **us**, we learn from them, and we pass on all the accumulated knowledge.

This industry of vaping and e-cigarettes is in transition and will be going through a lot more in the next several years. As a "highly unemployable entrepreneur" which is how I describe myself, I dedicated my time and energy towards guiding new business owners through this maze of changes over the past several years. I am a Baby Boomer who has been living this entrepreneurial life for four decades and has endured three recessions; I understand change. I never embraced the volatility but I do embrace the opportunities it affords. As I have shared with many, business is risky and the Vape Space is more risky than most. Nothing would trouble me more than to see a twenty-something start a Vape shop, have it fail and conclude "Well I guess it's back to Starbucks; this entrepreneurship thing is not for me."

Not going to happen on my watch.

I am the first to admit that in the world of vaping I am NOT a "technician." I don't tear stuff apart and put them back together and I do not vape so can only appreciate the wonderful juices by their smells, not by their tastes or the quality of their throat hits. By not being a vaper I remain 100% objective and unbiased when someone asked what mod I use or liquid I prefer. I am a **strategist** and after working with hundreds of different businesses in many, many fields I understand business and people and **that** is what creates success or failure in this industry.

Much of what I know I learned from my past mentors and work associates and for all of them, thank you again. As far as this new industry, this Brave New World where I am firmly entrenched, I thank all of you that taught and helped me as well. To my friends and associates that edited this work and gave me wonderful suggestions, well, could not have done it without you.

As I started my venture in July, 2013 I had no idea of whether I could offer anything to those in the industry or getting in. I bounced ideas off some that I respected and they helped me hone my business, my message and my deliverables. Thank you Julie Stone and Diane Lewis for your friendship and support as I ventured into unknown territory and made it to the other side. Just one year after "accidentally" walking into my first Vape shop I now have the privilege of consulting nationwide, speaking at expos and events throughout the country, plus get a chance to share my voice with Vape News Magazine, Vape News Radio, Tobacco International magazine and many blog posts. Thank you Matt Schramel, editor of Vape News, for the chance to share what I have.

This industry is lacking in many hard facts and we at VapeMentors strive to provide what you and everyone else needs and appreciates: Content. Blogging on E-Cig Media and Steve K's sites allow an outlet for sharing, along with interviews we have conducted with media outlets nationwide in all forms.

My first book was about failure; how to avoid it, how to recover from it. This book is about **SUCCESS:** how to attain it more assuredly, with less hassles and more fun. If you are still with me, keep reading, learn what I discovered, thank you and I wish you a long strange trip as well! Keep on Truckin'!

The past, the present, and the future, both of the industry—and of you (AKA Table of Contents)

Introduction   page 8

Chapter I
Where we started once upon a time…   page 16

Chapter II
Where we are now…   page 33

Chapter III
Where we are going (maybe…)   page 40

Chapter IV
Where are YOU??   page 43

Chapter V
What's your story?   page 71

Chapter VI
The "Personal Development" side of business and entrepreneurship.   page 78

Chapter VII
Creating your future in the Vape Space   page 86

Appendix
A Historical Timeline of Electronic Cigarettes   page 106

Introduction:

Sorry this book is so late. Just when I thought it was "up to date" things would change and staying on top of the dynamic vaping industry is like hitting a moving target. And not just a slowly moving target, like at an arcade or carnival, but like trying to hit a bullet in flight.

As I move into my second year within the vaping business I have witnessed amazing changes. Some for the better, some not so much. And of this you can be sure: this industry will continually **evolve** and change and you must stay **involved** if you want to ride this wild horse.

Who are you? Are you a casual or more user of e-cigarettes or vaping products? Are you "in the business" in whatever form that takes? Maybe you own (or want to own) a brick & mortar retail location. Maybe you intend to or already have an online store? Or possibly your vision is more grandiose: to develop your own lines of e-liquids or mechanicals or possibly multiple brick & mortar locations??

Regardless of which of these options applies to you, this book, this guide is made *for* **you**. It is not about me or my company, though it resonates from my personal vision and mission, along with forty years of entrepreneurial insight. More about my background and qualifications a bit later.

So here's the plan: By the time you read this book some of the information will have changed. The most significant adjustments being made right now:

Government intervention:

- That comes from the top down, which means the Federal Drug Administration—the FDA-- and individual states as well. Seems a bit ironic, doesn't it, that an agency that regulates drugs and food is now regulating vaping e-liquid and e-cigs, right?? The big sticking point is the "nicotine" issue since vaping products may contain it, though it is not based on tobacco. But really the biggest headaches you'll be dealing with for now is local politics, i.e., city councils and local restrictions. As we speak, some of the most major and significant cities in the nation, like New York, Boston, Chicago, and Los Angeles have new laws restricting vaping in public, the most obvious and intrusive pain in the ass. Sales to minors (under 18) are restricted, which we support, and there is lots of heat with permitting and zoning challenges as to where (if at all) you locate your retail store. We've dealt with more city governments regarding vaping shops than anyone in the country and understand their logic and rational. Many times they are both missing. More on that later.

The FDA:

- They are without a doubt the biggest "elephant in the room" and over time will have the most far reaching effect on the industry. As of this 2014 writing the FDA hearings are in process and we have in place what have been called the "Deeming Regulations." Look up "deeming" but in essence it just means that these are proposed and pending and are guidelines and insight to their way of thinking. Study them. These are discussion and battle zones which will have a huge impact on our futures.

The FDA has some legitimacy for what they are doing and some things that they need not get involved with. More on that later as well.

The state of the market, i.e. explosive growth and changing demographics:

- If we look back to the Big Bang of when it all "started" it wasn't that long ago. We'll bypass the ancient history of the first patent of a very primitive electronic cigarette from the 1960s and just focus on what happened in this century, post 2000. There were early attempts of duplicating what a cigarette *does*, which is deliver nicotine, one of the most highly addictive substances on the planet. It had varying degrees of success—and satisfaction. Truth is, this is part science but more art. Those that smoke are very particular and want the **satisfaction** of smoking and not just duplicate the "process," i.e., taking a drag, inhaling smoke (and nicotine), then exhaling. Repeating those steps may not be enough. The flavoring, the smell, the draw, the weight; they all must hit that sweet spot or there will be no permanent adoption.

    There is also more here than just nicotine dependency. If that were the case, patches and gum and hypnosis and other cessation methods would be more effective, but historically the "stickiness" of those alternatives is very low. Nicotine and tobacco addiction is more expensive on society than drugs, alcohol, gambling and every other addiction category and causes over $100B in added health related costs every year. Weaning off is part psychological, part physiological and part learned behavior.

This last step is the one that WE, those in the Vape Space, have the most control over. The FDA will do what they do when they do it and governments will react to those directions after much scrutiny and legal directions. We consider ourselves part of that "we" and between VapeMentors, Vape News Magazine and Vape News Radio, our mission is to find all the "we's" out there that wish to support freedom of choice and the right to make our own decisions.

There is yet another player that was late to the party but is making a huge impact regardless: **Big Tobacco**. Who or what is Big Tobacco?

Primarily "they" consist of three major companies: Altria, Lorillard, and RJ Reynolds. As of this writing a consolidation may be taking place and we may have just two major players. Any time you have "major players" in a broad based industry the leaders will emerge: Big Auto, Big Media, Big Oil. The names may change and their influence may ebb and flow, but most multi or deca billion dollar industries will have key influencers and we have ours.

So where does that leave you, Mr. (or Ms.) Vapreneur? Have you any influence, any power over the industry itself and over your small piece of the universe? You absolutely do.

A couple of key concepts and foundations I want to establish right now:

The definition of **Vapreneur**:

The world of "entrepreneurship" just a few decades ago was limited, not identified or defined and not supported to any large degree. Those days are no longer. Once upon a time, let's say back in the 1960's through the eighties, the word entrepreneur really didn't have much exposure nor was identified by the average person. The world got "smaller" in the 1980s due to technology, along with the "flattening of the earth" due to the opening up of China to the rest of the world and the fall of communism and the freeing of most Eastern Block countries. When you mix in the new generation that came *after* the Baby Boomers, the Gen X's and combine these factors, they all helped create a new mindset and one of the results was entrepreneurship. There is no lack of support in the space, either. There are groups that support women, Millennials (young entrepreneurs), and even younger, as in teens. All the various ethnic categories you can think of are covered and they all have groups specific and dedicated to empowerment.

What is and who is an entrepreneur? Typically those of us that are "highly unemployable," like to think outside the box, like to "take control," change the world and leave their mark or legacy fit that description. This book is about you, and certainly me. Most of us are BORN this way, always questioning, always seeking new opportunities and ways to do things differently; better.

The word entrepreneur has many derivations, and one of the most common is "solopreneur" which is a mash up of two words which are quite obvious. Most entrepreneurs are solopreneurs though many times do not identify themselves that way. They usually work alone, without a team, most times from a home base and usually have limited success. Of course there are countless exceptions, so give me some leeway here to make a point.

The majority of solopreneurs have a hard time with expansion, scalability, and outsourcing services or delegating. They usually are limited by attitude (I know how to do this, so it's easier/ faster for me to do it myself), or by budget. Typically there is a ceiling of how far they can go and to what degree of success they can reach. To find multi-million dollar companies run by solopreneurs are the exception and not the rule. Most will fall into the "barely getting by" revenue stage to maybe $500,000 annual revenue. When you get beyond one half million dollars you should shift your mindset, develop a team, create a business model or plan and look for expansion possibilities.

Another subset of solopreneurs are those that are called "lifestyle" solopreneurs. These are the mostly young people that work remotely, virtually and do not intend or want to create a larger company with many employees. Instead they develop apps, blog, write, and a host of other things that they can do anywhere with a laptop or tablet. In many cases they may generate very high income and are autonomous and self-sufficient. When you get a "hive" of folks like this together you can create a group of few to many, all working wherever and whenever they want, on their own schedule, but dedicated to a joint mission or vision. They are accountable to themselves, but more important, to each other and the collective mission they all create.

I coined the word **Vapreneur** as a mashup of entrepreneur and vaping. Shocker, right? It's a made up word but the person that wears that label is very real. It is me. It is most of my clients. It may be you.

The vaping world initially was very forgiving of naivety or lack of experience or providing good service. Initially captured and dominated by the "Millennial" or Gen Y generation (born about 1980-early 90's) this demographic is now facing a type of implosion after hitting a critical mass. That does not mean they--or you-- cannot survive and succeed in the Vape Space but the demographic model is changing and skewing towards an older, more experienced and more wealthy generation. Actually plural: **generations**. The Gen X'ers, who were born about 1964 (post Boomers) to about 1982 have come into the Vape Space in a big way. Their motivation is mostly the same but have huge differences from the Millennials. They carry some experience, maturity, access to capital and a passion that is different than the younger generation. They are looking for a lifestyle business if they came out of a corporate world, or maybe they have been an entrepreneur for many years. If they smoke or smoked they also may be seeing the damage they have wrought on their bodies and if they have kids they do not want to subject them to second-hand smoke.

And the last generation, the Baby Boomers, what used to be called the "Largest Generational Tidal Wave in History," is also creeping into the Vape Space. Those Boomers, born from 1946-1964 have their own motivation for getting into vaping and they are a force to be reckoned with. Smart, seasoned, experienced, and with access to capital, the Boomers are making huge strides into the vaping industry. True they lack social media and tech skills—and usually lack specifics within the hardware/ e-liquid conversation—but they have worked around those limitations. They hire them. It is much easier to hire technicians than to find seasoned, experienced entrepreneurs. Sometimes they have a great vision and plan to change since many times vaping or e-cigs allowed them to stop smoking after decades and other programs that did not stick. Female Boomers are making a strong showing and we have a special report on that.

Since these worlds are changing so rapidly this book is not designed to be a "final product" but IS designed to be the basis and foundation to the Ultimate Guide to the Vaping Business.

Every calendar quarter we will be putting out updates that address all we just mentioned, from the FDA to impact of government to the changing face and demographics of the vaping industry.

These will be subscription based with the next edition scheduled during Q1 2015. Stay tuned and be watching.

Oh, and by the way, inserted within this book are three "Easter Eggs" and if you ever played video or online games you know what they are. If you identify all three Easter Eggs, send us a note to sales@VapeMentors.com with the subject line "Easter Eggs." Winner gets free bling!

Chapter ONE: Where we started once upon a time...

The saying goes "those that do not study the past are doomed to repeat it." This comes from developed war strategies along with understanding how to deal with people in all segments and walks of life. When you boil it down to basics, we are all the same with the same wants and needs. And if you really want to command **your** space you absolutely must study the past, but more important you must study the present—the NOW—especially in your particular world. The Vape Space is international and national in broad scope but 95% of all that is outside your control, which is awesome! That means you only need to worry about your little slice of heaven. How big or how small that is, is very personal to you and your business model.

You do not need to go back too far in time nor delve too deeply unless you choose to be a student so that is a personal decision. If you are serious about being a Vapreneur then it's in our/your best interest to be a student of the industry and know a little about a lot and a **lot** about your particular field or market.

A brief timetable of where this industry came from over the past several years is in the back, The Appendix, primarily since many of you may not want to read it right now. I suggest you do so, regardless. Much of it came courtesy of www.CASAA.org and www.SFATA.org, two advocacy groups I support and suggest you do as well. These organizations are our eyes and ears and many times our **voices** of the industry. (E-cigarette History: http://casaa.org/E-cigarette_History.html)

Another group you should know about, to reference at a minimum, is the American Council on Science and Health.

(www.acsh.org). This started as a group of scientists that in 1978 started asking questions about public health and safety policies that were **not** based on "pure scientific principles." Ironic that three and one half decades later that same concern still exists. Common sense in this Vape Space is not so common.

I suggest you take a look at their history, but in brief, here's the background from their site:

"ACSH's mission is to ensure that peer-reviewed mainstream science reaches the public, the media, and the decision-makers who determine public policy. The objective is to restore science and *common sense* to personal and public health decisions in order to foster a scientifically sound and sensible public health policy for the American people and ACSH is committed to improving communication and dialogue between the scientific/medical community and the public and the media, in an effort to ensure that the coverage of health issues is based on scientific **facts** – not hyperbole, emotion or ideology." (Highlights are mine)

The nucleus of ACSH is a board of 350 physicians, scientists and policy advisors — experts in a wide variety of fields — who review the Council's reports and participate in ACSH seminars, media communications, and other educational activities.

ACSH is continually active in the public sphere: Council representatives appear regularly on television and radio, in public debates, and in other forums. In addition, ACSH hosts media seminars and press conferences on a variety of public health issues. ACSH also provides an in-house internship program for students in health science fields and participates in legislative and regulatory hearings." (ref: http://acsh.org/about-acsh/)

Since I know the short attention span of many these days (myself included) I have supplied a pictorial history that is easier to understand and follow for the less patient called "***A Visual History of e-cigarettes and Vaping.***"

The quick snapshot:

Once upon a time there was...Nothingness

And then came...tobacco (Thank you American Indians) and the joy (or habit) of smoking...

Which grew into an Industry... a very profitable industry! Television took over from print and radio marketing and dominated the advertising world for years, along with the TV set. Thank you Madison Avenue and the "Mad Men" that brainwashed America.

Fast forward to the new and improved alternatives to "analog" cigarettes! Thank you Hon Lik. (NOTE: He actually took the idea from an American who patented the original in the early 1960's.

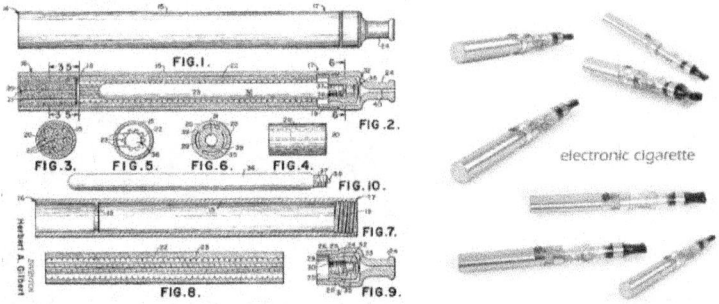

And then there was Vape...and smoking has never been the same.

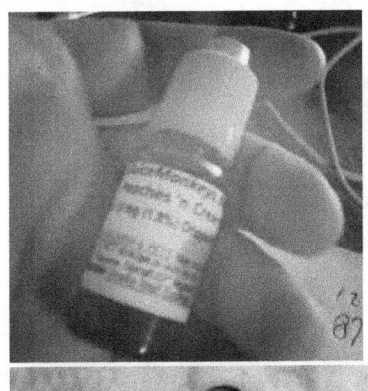

Today you have multiple players, channels and industry silos:

"Big Tobacco"

E-cig manufacturers:

Vape E-liquid manufacturers:

Brick & Mortar stores, online stores, etc...

And the battle for survival continues today between all these players and those that wish to regulate...

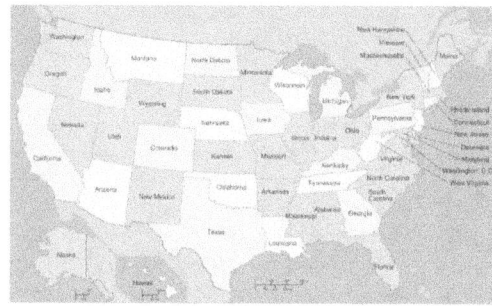

The worse of them all...

Local politicians, cities of all sizes, and their lack of information...

The Future...

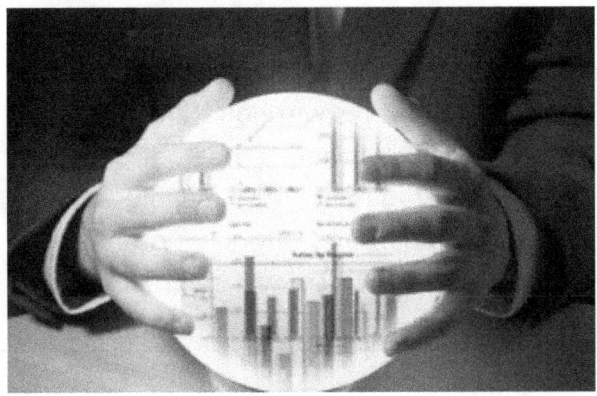

More:

- Regulation
- Taxation
- Growth of the market with e-cigs, Vape shops, e-liquid manufacturers (until the FDA issues final guidelines, so that may change)
- Adaptation of short and long-term smokers to digital smoking options
- Changing demographics of users and business owners, both skewing towards older demographics

Breaking news:

As we are ready to print, some big news was announced as Lorillard has agreed to sell the "blu" e-cigarette line, to Imperial, a U.K. based cigarette manufacturer, for $7.1 Billion dollars. This shedding of blu was expected but all eyes were on RJ Reynolds as the purchaser, so this purchase, which includes the Kool, Salem and Winston brands as well, caught many by surprise. blu is the largest e-cigarette seller on the market and this now potentially creates a new "Big Tobacco" player. The deal will be finalized sometime in 2015

The Here and Now

There have been states that forbid vaping in public, cities following suit and controversy galore over whether the product is:

a) A tobacco product
b) NOT a tobacco product
c) A drug delivery device

These fights will continue until the FDA hearings conclude, but we are just halfway through the nine step process until it becomes **law**. Ironically there is even controversy within our own industry as to what this product "is." Is a vaping e-liquid a tobacco product, subject to the same laws and regs and taxation of conventional tobacco?" Many say yes- others disagree.

I encourage you to support CASAA (another mouthful, this stands for "**Consumer Advocates for Smoke-free Alternatives Association**) which is primarily an advocacy group that informs their subscribers of all the new events that can impact our industry, usually negative events. Is your city or a city close to you threatening a city council vote to outlaw outdoor vaping? CASAA usually knows about it, shares the word, and encourages you and every other fan to rally in support and opposition. My first introduction to CASAA involved a local Orange County (CA) city, Seal Beach, and the efforts of a new Vape shop owner to fight city hall.

This young man had a vision, a dream. He was going to open a Vape shop in this pretty, quiet seaside town. For Orange County this *is* the definition of a small town, with a population of about 25,000 and just 13 sq. miles.

He and his fiancée did everything right. They applied for and got a business license. They applied for and got a building permit on a beautiful location along the main route going right through town and just blocks from the ocean. Small strip center, good walking traffic as well as a good traffic count. So far so good, right?

They had their lease in hand, started working on the TI (tenant improvements) and were denied a permit to continue. They reached out to CASAA for help and CASAA brought me into the picture since I had a background of working with cities, mayors and councils. The city had NO legitimate reason to stop the permit process other than that they **could**. This industry is controversial, contentious and cities many times take an extreme position to cover their asses from liabilities and that's what happened here.

Their concern: There were "too many" Vape shops and distributors in this town. They did not want to support the "bad element" of vaping.

 Maybe there *were* too many shops but at that time there were few stand-alone dedicated Vape shops and most vape sales were down at convenience stores and the like. Were they right in being concerned? That's a matter of opinion but the only opinion that mattered was that of the city council. They road-blocked the permit and deferred a decision to the next city council meeting which was weeks away. Meanwhile Mr. Pending Vapreneur is responsible for the lease on a location he cannot occupy nor work on.

The city's first step was a moratorium, a very common ploy to defer any final decisions, so they issued a moratorium for 13 months. Crazy right? They wanted our Vapreneur to sit idly by for over a year until the city could make a final ruling. They backed off on that and decided to have a hearing the following month instead. The "plaintiff" as I'll call him, went in prepared. He had legal standings and precedent, along with an army of members of the public that *supported* his business. No one opposed this shop except for the city. The city ruled and reduced the 13 month moratorium but still made it impractical for our friend to wait around until they reversed their ruling, and even that was not guaranteed.

The net result was that our budding business owner was out almost $50K, disillusioned with his city and the industry and left the city as well as the state.

This sounds like an extreme example, unlikely to be duplicated, right?? **Wrong**. This scenario with various components and various outcomes has been played out many times nationally. There are lessons to be learned here and as that saying goes, "study the past," so this is a glaring example of what that refers to.

First rule, never, *ever* to be broken: be sure you get permission, permits and a license (or at least something in writing that says they will approve you) before you find a location. That is not a guarantee you will be able to proceed but it goes a long, long way. Do your research and know that there absolutely are shortcuts which we can share with you.

Is there a current shop in town? A good indication you'll be approved, but not guaranteed. Are you in a "larger" town, in excess of 100,000 residents? More likely to be approved. Bigger towns are more business friendly (not a hard, fast rule) and are less ruled by arrogance and egos. Smaller towns, especially those with a **real** home town vibe, may be troublesome. They are sometimes ruled by the will of just a few and if those few don't want "that kind of business in our town," don't fight it, just move on.

An observation based on recent experiences.

Vaping and e-cigs are very controversial, which is obvious. The connections to tobacco and other "sinners' vices" are also not a stretch of the imagination. I have personally gotten negative pushback from friends and associates that took issue with me being in "this industry." That didn't and doesn't stop me but it may others.

There are parts of this country that are considered more conservative, more religious, and more puritanical: you can put on whatever label you like. You would think that Vape shops would be disdained and looked down upon in those areas that follow that religious pattern but I am seeing the Vape shops—including conventions and conferences—making headway into even some of the most puritanical areas like New England and notably the state of Utah, which is a primarily Latter Day Saints (Mormon) territory. Does that mean you will automatically be given a heroes' welcome in those areas and given the keys to the city? Does that mean trying to start a business in a "larger" town is a given? The answer is NO to both. Every situation is different and you should create a **plan**, a **model** and develop a proposal letter for cities' zoning and permitting departments as well as for landlords who also can be anti-vape shop. We have templates available for both.

A bit about SFATA.org, which stands for "**Smoke-free Alternatives Trade Association**." I know, I have a problem with that mouthful and have discussed it with their Executive Director. We'll see if they do a name change and rebranding as this industry continues to grow.

As CASAA is an advocacy group and watchdog, SFATA does similar with more focus on the industry for business practices. You hear the term "Best Practices" which most industries try to follow, though it may be challenging to define what it really means. In essence it means that businesses do things in an ethical, moral, effective, efficient and fair way. That crosses over into how the employees are treated as well as vendors and especially clients and customers.

SFATA keeps an eye on the industry but they also keep an eye on US. Are we doing the right thing and following good business practices? Are we being fair to the industry and not bringing a negative aspect to us? SFATA keeps a watchful eye over us and sometimes in spite of ourselves.

Aside from regulators and advocacy groups our biggest watchdogs and our greatest strengths are ourselves—our industry. We must police (hate that word) ourselves and watch over each other. One bad company or poor business practice can upend the entire industry and believe me, we have watchers keeping an eye on *everything* we do. As much as the FDA and government are just waiting to catch us doing things wrong or poorly our biggest challenge and the one we must be *most* mindful of is The Media.

WHO is The Media? It's the TV stations and news stations and radio and all forms of digital and written disseminations from newspapers, magazines, both online and hard copy and blogs and bloggers. They all want their 15 minutes of fame and would love to catch us doing something wrong. The media needs very little incentive to publicize any bad that happens and rarely gives us fair and equitable treatment. Some examples:

- "Children get sick on open Vape e-liquid bottle"
    Yes it's true, it has happened, but more kids get sick on alcohol, drugs of all type, cleaning products or chemicals, etc… and we don't see the same backlash. Kids can ingest anything that is within the reach of their mouths, so be aware of the negative publicity. And if you have kids, please keep all your devices and e-liquid out of their reach. Consider it a safer, though dangerous, firearm and use caution.
- "High school kids caught with vaping pen in school"
    Yes, this is true, too, and you can be sure kids are caught with drugs, alcohol, stolen goods

and firearms. Teens have been pushing boundaries and breaking laws long before I got caught smoking pot in high school... Heck, isn't that why they called it that?

- "Homemade vaping juice manufactured with no standardization"

    Wow, this is true as well. The industry overall **wants** standardization and there are groups like AEMSA, which stands for **The American E-liquid Manufacturing Standards Associate** (http://www.aemsa.org/) which helps monitor it. The irony is that all the issues of the media have legitimate foundations that the industry itself is aware of. We are doing what we can to overcome those challenges. Easter Egg #1: What does the acronym AEMSA stand for?

- "E-cigarette battery explodes and a) causes fire, b) blows leg off small child or c) kills family's pet dog"

    Take your pick, I have seen them all. Anytime you deal with electricity you risk problems and you don't need to look very far to find other examples like Dell laptops batteries melting down or electric cars, including Fisker, Chevrolet or Tesla batteries all causing fire.

These problems happen so rarely (like plane crashes) that media jumps all over it and makes into something bigger than what it is.

The lessons to be learned? Be careful, don't buy into the hype and deal with emotional hyperbole with facts.

Chapter TWO: Where we are now…

Now that we know where we've been, let's get a look at where we are today. That of course has many facets and this book is designed to keep you apprised of **today** with successive installments. For simplicity sake we'll go back to our overview in the introduction and focus on:

- The FDA
- Government actions and interventions
- The "Market"
- Big Tobacco

The FDA (Food & Drug Administration) is the government agency under the Department of Health and Human Services (one of the executive departments) designed to monitor, police and regulate the food and "drugs" we put in our bodies. They started in 1906 as part of the Food and Drug Act, and they carry a lot of power. One of their primary missions is to monitor and force standardization of food and drug products and to eliminate false or misleading boasts or claims. They are also very contradictory.

Can you sell vitamin *supplements* that are totally unregulated and can possibly cause unknown side effects when ingested? The answer is "yes" and they are legal as long as the manufacturer makes no **medical** claims and does not offer unsubstantiated claims of benefits. Will it help you lose weight? Sure. Suppress your appetite? Why not? The placebo effect is very powerful in the supplement industry and consumers lose countless billions of dollars every year due to bogus produces. Fortunately there are few deaths, but for the most part that industry is a Wild West circus.

No doubt you hear and read advertisements for drugs on TV and magazines and papers. In many cases the side effects are enough to cause you to avoid this new Wonder Drug, but the process that was required to get that particular drug to market took tens if not hundreds of millions of dollars and many years. Is the FDA necessary? I believe so, and like any government agency run by people it is far from perfect and unfortunately they do not always have their facts in hand.

And that leaves vaping...

Is it a tobacco product? Is there tobacco **IN** it? What about nicotine? Is it "safe?"

These are the questions that the FDA is tasked to address and there are talking points on both sides. A longer dialogue of this discussion will be in successive books and updates to this book, but for the most part there are no clear cut answers to most questions. Even so, here is where the FDA seems to be going:

- NO sales to minors
- NO restriction on internet sales
- NO freebie giveaways of products
- NO ban on advertising

We could spend pages dissecting the novel sized report they released but the consensus of legal and advocacy watchdogs is that no final decision will be forthcoming in 2014 and it is doubtful if we'll see any conclusions in 2015, either.

Those key points above are the easy ones. Here's where it gets tricky and head scratchy.

- Sales of products that were developed and originated after February 15, 2008, must be *individually* approved by the FDA. I wanted this to be an easy to read overview and guide and not get bogged down in legalese, but if you'd like to review here are some links:

- http://www.fda.gov/TobaccoProducts/Labeling/ucm388395.htm
- http://casaa.org/
- http://sfata.org/blog/2014/04/25/for-immediate-release-fda-deeming-regulations-424/

Say what?

For the consumer and most Vape Shops these rules are easy to follow but the last point is controversial and potentially a deal breaker.

Scenario:

You manufacture e-liquid. Ten flavors, four nicotine levels, that's 40 SKU (stock keeping unit) numbers. A SKU is the smallest identifier an individual sales item can be broken down by for sales tracking. Imagine that you sold nails of varying lengths of ¼", ½", with different dimensions, i.e., thicknesses. Every one of each size is its own SKU. So to bring it back to our liquids, every one of your 40 e-liquids would have its own SKU, even though all your nic levels could be the **same**.

If you were to take them in for testing it could run into hundreds of hours of paperwork and tens of thousands of dollars to get *each one* of your items 40 approved. Time consuming, onerous, expensive. An inane system which will probably be modified in its final forms. Who knows?

The Line(s) in the Sand: Vape vs. E-cigs

Do not think this is a war since we are all on the same side (more or less), but there is a distinction between these two very different models. Do you or do you wish to carry e-cigs 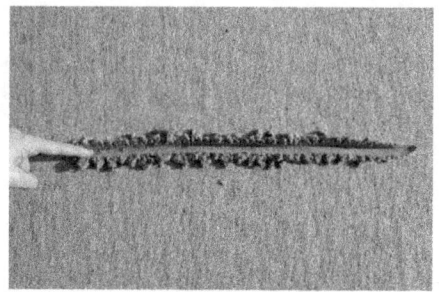 or strictly stay with mods, tanks and liquids? Most of you probably will stay with plan B, but there is a definite movement from traditional Smoke Shops that are expanding or moving into vape products and there are some stores that actually benefit from carrying both.

The e-cig movement took off with great speed and accelerated when Big Tobacco finally realized they were losing money and jumped in with both feet. As of this writing the e-cig space is undergoing significant changes.

Lorillard (stock ticker LO, named after the founder, Pierre Lorillard in 1760) in 2012 bought blu (note, all lower case) for $135M and within a year they commanded nearly half the market and everyone else was playing catch up.

In summer, 2014 Lorillard agreed to be purchased by Reynolds American for $27.4B which was a transaction that was watched and expected. What was not fully anticipated was that before the sale Lorillard sold blu off as a separate entity to Imperial tobacco (Big Tobacco #4) to bypass any possible antitrust (monopoly) issues. This is a hugely complex transaction with multiple players and would not be finalized until 2015.

Altria (ticker MO, since it is the parent company of Phillip **Mo**rris tobacco, a former big player in itself) is currently #1 in the Big Tobacco world. As big ships are hard to turn and navigate, this big ship is the last to the e-cigarette party. They purchased one of the bigger e-cig companies, Green Smoke, in 2014 and are rolling out their own product called "MarkTen" (all one word) this year.

Why is this all important? Because if you are to succeed in this industry you should have a good "30,000 foot view" of all the players and the entire landscape.

Altria owns some of the most iconic names in the tobacco industry, such as Marlboro, Copenhagen, Skoal, and command over 50% of the entire market share. These industries are centuries old and have been part of the American culture almost since our founding over 300 years ago. For decades Big Tobacco was a major player in our *lives*, our cultures, our worlds and certainly our televisions and other media. This transition of analog tobacco to digital is beyond huge and the effects on this industry cannot be overstated. We are witnessing history and the total evolution of one of the biggest industries in the world.

Reynolds American did something unique in that instead of buying their own e-cig lines they created one from scratch: Vuse. They are doing national rollouts in 2014 and should be nationwide by the end of the year. This was a big move since they started from scratch, researched what worked and what didn't; what people liked and what they disliked, and started with a clean slate.

Other players that are not "Big" but should be noted include Logic, the largest of the independents and NJOY, who recently rolled out their own lines of e-liquid.

Where will these Big Guys go in the future?

The irony behind all this is that e-cigarette sales have declined since their previous highs and are losing market share. Granted they are increasing compared to the decline of analog cigarettes but the public which was once enamored with digital cigs are losing their taste (literally), primarily because they don't satisfy or feel the same and to truly change habits and addictive behavior takes more than just one piece of the puzzle.

As e-cigs sales are dropping, conversion to vaping is very high. *This cannot be ignored and is a sign of things to come*. And where you may fit in.

The "Global Scenario"

If we look at vaping and e-cigs on a global scale, this is Big Business and getting bigger. As challenging as the FDA is to work with, some countries have instituted even more stringent bans and respected organizations like the Geneva-based World Health Organization is not a proponent. In their very conservative eyes they look at this industry as a public health hazard and regardless of what we do and how the FDA rules here, the overseas battle will be more challenging.

The world's largest markets are North America and Europe and of the 59 countries that currently regulate the device, 13 ban them outright. Even so, Black Markets exist and will always be available for anyone that wants anything. As an example of how slow regulators move, even on this scale, WHO is scheduled to have a conference in Fall, 2014 which they committed to having as early as 2012. They want all countries to tighten up their guidelines and universally restrict sales to anyone under age 18.

If you are curious as to how many e-cigarette brands exist internationally the number pegged is **466** and you can be sure that number will crest 500 by the time you read this.

Chapter THREE: Where we are going (maybe...)

Of these facts you can be sure: the Vaping industry is not going away, regardless of the FDA or states or cities, and this market will exist for years or decades to come. Following that prediction is my second one which states that this market will be going through *constant* changes, both small and large for the foreseeable future.

As we've stated, "Those that do not study history are doomed to repeat it." It typically refers to political or war strategies and points out that many lessons, both negative and positive, have already been learned and do not need to be experienced to move forward. That premise applies in your life as well.

Even though the "business" of vaping and Vape shops is new, and there are few metrics or statistics to learn from, but when you drill businesses down to their core, most are all the same. All businesses want higher revenue, lower costs, better customer service, more streamlined operations, and so forth. Most businesses differ by about 20% and that is primarily due to their core offering, whether a service or some type of product. When you take that down one more level, what makes one Vape shop different than another? If you use numbers, it's that 10% difference between the winners and the losers, between the super successful and the marginally profitable that matter. **How** you differentiate yourself is key and surprisingly easy to identify, though maybe more difficult to execute.

I have found that most of us, entrepreneurs or not, have good intentions but lack in execution. We know we should be doing this or that or the next thing, but guess what happens?

Life happens, things get in the way and great planning does not get carried forth.

Here are some key opportunities in the Vape Space going forward:

- Opening a brick & mortar retail location
- Developing an online store
- Offering "other" components or products
- Affiliate programs if you have good web traffic
- Your own line of e-liquid or for others

These will be addressed shortly.

The question of Big Tobacco comes up repeatedly. I have spoken with all of these companies along with many e-cig companies and many e-liquid manufacturers. My personal opinion is that we are all on the same side of the argument and we all want *regulation*, but we do not want **restrictions**.

We all believe that standardizing the manufacturing processes will benefit all involved and we will see the dust settle in the next few years. Many cities and states point to the FDA for answers since they do not know nor do they wish to take personal responsibly for such a far reaching industry.

Big Tobacco brings years of experience in lobbying and influence peddling (used here as a compliment…) and they have billions of dollars at risk. The rate of analog cigarette smoking has dropped annually and they see just one future ahead: electronic cigarettes, AKA e-cigs.

Based on consolidation, reinvention and invention they have and will pour tens of billions of dollars annually into research, advertising and court room battles. For right now I view Big Tobacco as our ally, but see the day approaching when they may become our competition and adversaries. Vaping rides on their coattails so enjoy the ride.

We have interviewed several of the "major players" in the Vape Space on Vape News Radio and the RJ Reynolds Vapors interview can be heard here: http://vapenewsradio.podbean.com/e/imran-khan-interview-part-2-contests/

A second interview with RJ Reynolds Vapor is pending and can be heard at www.VapeNewsRadio.com.

Upcoming is an interview with NJOY and several other big names.

Chapter FOUR: Where are YOU??

There are several ways to get IN to the Vape Space.

BRICK AND MORTAR

How many brick and mortar stores (retail shops) do we have in the country? 3000? 5000? 8634? More than 10,000? I've heard all these numbers bandied about (not the 8634, though…) and truth is no one knows. Virtually since my Day One, when I walked into my first shop in Newport Beach, California on July 4, 2013 and asked "What the hell is a Vape Shop?," I have been putting together metrics. Initially none existed, as in ZERO! I had to create relationships and dig into data bases and even now I still don't know the exact number and have gotten great support from VapeFinds, who you will meet shortly. We'll never have any definite answers and probably never will since it is that dynamic. This is still a fragmented industry run by mostly new business owners that do **not** like to play or speak with each other. Most have a selfish "ME" attitude and are unlikely to share any intel. Another question is, "What does a Vape Shop really look like?"

Is a stand-alone kiosk part of the census? How about a store that sells other things and also sells some e-liquid as well? Swap meet booths? Some smoke shops sell e-liquid; should they be counted? How about convenience stores and Wal-Marts and Costcos that sell e-cigs but (currently) no e-liquid products. This is why you hear a large range of estimates from 5,000 to over 35,000. There are more questions than answers.

I've recently dissected the industry and broken them down into seven broad categories. An excerpt from my report:

The Definitive Guide to Vape Shops

A.   Vape Shops: these are pure focused shops dedicated to newbies, offering starter kits, hardware, e-liquids of many types and flavors, usually a tasting bar, information, support and hand holding. On the other end they cater to the experts and hobbyists that can tear apart a mod with their eyes closed as though they were in boot camp dismantling an M-16 rifle. How many are there? Indications and directories available total about 6,000-7,000 TRUE Vape Shops. That number has come from multiple sources and until anyone proves otherwise I'm going with it.

B.   Smoke Shops: these started out as exclusive stores catering to smokers and offered cigarettes and tobacco in all forms, all analog, and most, about 60-75%, are now adding vaping products to their list. They are usually light on knowledge and serve a captive audience that comes in for one thing and may leave with another. They would be heavier in the e-cig/ closed system segment as opposed to the juice, but due to generous profit margins, that is shifting. Many of them have a loyal following so that helps the conversion to digital smoking products.

C.   Hybrids: these are stores that offer vape products but also sell other things. It could be a clothing store or something not related to smoking or e-liquid markets at all. They see an opportunity and are there strictly to offer products, period; just a point of sale. This can also include hookah lounges unless they strongly cater to the VTM, Vapor/ Tank/ Mod market and if half their revenue is generated by these products I would put them in category "B" with Smoke Shops.

D.   Head shops: you know what they are, we know what they are. Everyone knows, but for legal purposes they sell, "smoking devices" to be used for legal products only, i.e., no marijuana. Exceptions right now are Colorado and Washington State. Head shops have been around since the 60's and they offer vaping and e-cigs because, like smoke shops, they may have a captive and loyal audience.

E.   C-stores, or Convenience stores: these are the 7-11s, Circle K's, AM-PM mini markets, and a host of other national and regional shops. These are stores you rarely are in for more than 10 minutes. You fill up with gas, grab a pack of e-cigs, or now, possibly liquids, maybe a Milky Way bar or a Slurpee and you're on your way. They know little to nothing about the products and are a pure point of sale, but their sheer numbers make them noteworthy and a growing influencer.

F.   Retail drug and food stores: these are stores you go in to for shopping; maybe for food, maybe to fill a prescription, get some antiperspirant and personal products and "Hey, there's some juice! Let me try one of those and might as well throw in a starter kit, too." You may spend more time in this type of location but not as much as

G.   Mass market retailers: these are the Big Boys strictly in terms of physical size and stature in the business world. Costco sells e-cigs, as does Wal-Mart and Target stores plus many regional chains. Vaping products and liquids are just starting to intrude here and will be more prevalent as time goes by.

Who is the "average" Vape Shop owner and how did they start? Some generalities, but with exceptions:

- Usually former smokers who have quit and had a life changing epiphany and want to "save the world."
- Sometimes former smokers that are highly entrepreneurial and see a niche business.
- Many times Gen Y or Millennials (ages 20-32) that may have smoked or not, but love the social aspects of vaping.
- The new model: entrepreneurs that neither smoked nor vaped but see a lucrative business.

The market has been shifting towards older demographics both with users as well as shop owners and will continue in that direction. There is also a notable increase in women owned businesses and that will continue to grow as our Special Reports reveal.

So where do you fit in and how do you get there? Let's learn from those that did some things right and some things that could have been done differently.

Vapor Craze, Long Beach, CA (www.VaporCraze.net)

Jon Merton wanted to be a cop. He took courses and had a degree in Criminal Justice, but developed a cough that took that dream away. His military background and all the education he acquired meant nothing if he was not physically able to be a policeman. And the blame rested on his cigarette habit which he tried to kick every way he could until he was introduced to vaping and e-cigarettes in mid-2009. Jon was one of the early pioneers when this Wild West was even more wild, and there were less gunslingers and even fewer rules.

In the summer of 2009, Jon ran out of cigarettes (while at the gym no less), went into a convenience store and bought his first e-cig. It was a decent replacement for the cigarettes he so loved, but not enough to satisfy him to quit. He was OK with the replacement as an alternative but his curiosity was aroused and off to the internet he went to find something better and he found the world of "mods." Since he was a tinkerer he bought some items, dissected them and pieced them back together and started attending different vape meetings and met some of the very first pioneers in the industry. Mind you, they were making very small quantities of hardware and selling whatever they could make and for the most part there was no market for importing products from overseas.

He had a passion, saw that vaping was helping him, so he began selling products from his car trunk to people he would randomly meet at coffee shops, on the street or at the gym. He had just gotten out of college, 25 years old and was not able to continue his military career nor his police training. He was broke and saw a way to make some money. BTW, that is the mark of an entrepreneur: **find a need and fill it**.

He took orders, charged a 10% premium and got people what they wanted. He didn't get rich but that wasn't his agenda. His goal was to share his cure for smoking and now Karma came around in a good way since he was unknowingly on his way to a new career.

He found a local supplier and web shopping site in his home area of Southern California, called the owner and decided to meet this guy- Matt Woertler, the founder. They met and both realized that Jon had a lot more knowledge than Matt, but Matt had one of the first online businesses, so they decided to join forces and expanded the online store and tap into Jon's great depth of connections. Their first business model was simply brokering or "drop shipping" which required no inventory and minimal risk. Plowing all their minimal profits into the company in Q1 of 2010 they finally raised enough money to buy 50 starter kits, then 100, then 200 starter kits; their first inventory. Jon did the selling, Matt did the fulfillment and the profits increased, but with Matt holding a full time job, they soon reached capacity.

Jon's cousin by marriage, Joeffrey, had the time, had the interest and soon he joined them and was storing inventory at his home and shipping from there. Now the partnership was complete and continues to this day as they operated under the original name "310 Vapors," 310 being one of the most distinctive area codes in Los Angeles.

Starting with nothing, but with fate taking control, Matt was soon laid off from his job and forced them all to get serious; to form a legitimate company. After much discussion and planning they decided, with a great sense of fear and worry, to open their first retail location in Long Beach in the fall of 2010, and were just a few months behind the very first one that opened in Los Angeles. They held the first "Vape Meet" in Los Angeles and the store was a hit from day one as friends and family came to them and asked about franchising or partnering. Dismissing the franchising idea, (rightfully so) they soon opened four more stores with a licensing agreement and by charging a hefty start-up fee but no royalties, they were on their way to developing a mini-dynasty.

As the renamed Vapor Craze grew (from 310 Vapors), so did their presence in the marketplace and they befriended innovators within the industry which helped them become known as experts in the field.

Fast forward to today. Since then they have developed their own lines of e-liquids, created their own lab, and export to many overseas markets. They have also closed most of those other stores. As often happens, partnerships are prone to disintegration and deterioration and that is what happened here. Jon, Matt and Joeffrey remained intact, but many of their other relationships did not. Unreal or unfulfilled expectation, jealousy, greed; they all crept in and tore it all down.

Vapor Craze still exists and is not going anywhere, but like any (good) business, they have been open to change, and are in the process of reinventing (restructuring). They created many benchmarks in several areas plus created and promoted the largest and most well-attended vaping event in Southern California in October 2013, called Vapetoberfest.

With unexpected record crowds of more than 8000 people over two days, Vapetoberfest was fun, organized, and created many outcomes from that weekend event. I was invited to speak and that event helped launch VapeMentors to become what it is today. They will surely do another Vapetoberfest and of all the events I have been to, that one still stands tall due to their organization, their execution, the networking they provided and as important, the fun. They delivered!

What did they do right, where did they err, and what did they learn?

- They grew slowly, before they opened their very first store, very organically, which is the best way to grow, but requires something many do not have: patience.
- The partnership between Jon, Matt and Jeoffrey was formed by new relationships but was done with full transparency and in writing.
- When things went "off the track" they didn't bitch about it, they just cut their losses and refocused on a new direction.
- Even though they **did** grow slowly they did not screen their partners properly. The importance of this is significant since a weak partnership at the beginning will rarely end well. Vetting and training cannot be over stated.
- Today they are mostly distributors, not looking for, but not averse to opening new locations and are not looking to open anything in Southern California.
- One thing they did with a new focus was to design and manufacture their own branded starter kits. Now they have e-liquid, they have retail presence and they have hardware. From the outside looking in, those are hallmarks of a well-rounded company.

Vape Supreme, Fullerton, CA (www.VapeSupreme.com)

Lance Feliciano wanted to learn social media so he started working for a social media marketing company, but after a short time his entrepreneurial spirit kicked in and he decided to venture out on his own. After gathering several old friends, as in friends as far back as junior high and high school days, they all teamed up and started a Vape shop based on the suggestion of Lance's uncle. They were not familiar with the industry, so they researched and discovered that the **market** was *not* catering to the **marketplace**- nor to their generation, the Millennials. For two months they researched and looked for locations, driving the streets where Lance wanted to locate their retail store.

With his focus firmly on his tribe—the Millennials- and his background in social media, he knew this was the perfect strategy and the right target audience. At the "perfect" age of 24 Lance and his team had enough experience to do their homework and started Vape Supreme's first shop in Fullerton, California.

Like many beginners, Lance had no funds, so went back to his uncle and borrowed the money to open his shop. BTW, he did this on a handshake with no paperwork or agreement. Lance drove every street in the area he wanted to locate within, found the location and opened in December 2012.

With his prior experience as a party promoter in LA, plus their collective deep social media connections, his team ended up with an invite list of more than 5000 people for their Grand Opening, including two models with 100,000 Instagram followers each! Opening day was a zoo with streams of cars coming and going and from there on the store was a great success. Success breeds a lot of interest so people came to Lance and his team and inquired about franchising or expanding. They decided to **not** go that route but ended up opening four more stores, all with his original partners and close friends or family members.

This rise to success was explosive but one of the biggest realities in the risky entrepreneurial vape world is that the fall can be just as fast. In about 15 months their growth curve stopped but their overhead continued. And there was one more overlooked detail: the Tax Man, both federal and state. The last agency you want to piss off is the Franchise Tax Board (the California State Tax collector), who are worse than the IRS.

Lance was candid about what should have been done differently. They decided to "do their own thing" and some of it was good and some of it was not. Such is the nature of entrepreneurship. They created a unique mark by making "fashionable" hardware, including creating patterns on their custom vapeware.

They were cutting edge in their social media world and very significant with their competitive position, but just 18 months after they began they have effectively shut down their five stores and are refocusing on becoming a **brand** and not so focused on brick and mortar retail stores. They are paring down and creating their own products.

The lessons to be learned:

- Tap into your strengths and understand yourself.
- Study the market and find out how to cater to them
- Discover your "natural market"
- If you borrow money, make sure all agreements are in writing
- If you have partners, find those with a great trust factor
- Be careful about expanding too quickly
- If you have talents and skills in social media and marketing **use them.**
- If things aren't working find out **quickly** and change directions quickly
- Thinking big is a great idea; don't be afraid to try new things. Study the market and develop a strategy to dominate.
- Pay your taxes!!

And the final takeaways:

In Lance's words, "This experience turned boys into men," which I found very insightful, and "Just because you fail does not make you a failure." They had nothing when they started and the experience they gained was more valuable than any college education. They learned that "making money is an art," and I could not agree more.

The comparisons between these two companies are notable, yet they took different paths after finding out what needed to change. As an observer, adviser and participant in this growing vape industry these stories are not isolated cases at all, but are very typical of patterns I see. The "failure rate" right now is about 1:4 or 1:5 which means that for every four or five stores opening, one is closing down. I suspect the number of new stores will slow down a bit and the number of closings will stay consistent.

ONLINE

Online stores also take many different forms, some of them better (and more successful) than others. An online store is cheaper and probably easier from the standpoint of not needing a physical location, nor permits or employees, licenses, etc… It is also incredibly easy to do *poorly*, which goes across the board and certainly includes poorly run and poorly formatted brick and mortar locations. If you want to do this you should ideally have the skill sets to do the work yourself as opposed to contracting it out. Having experience in e-commerce and developing an online store is a big plus and fortunately there are great resources and tools to make this more viable than in years past.

An online business can take different forms, from being fairly traditional shopping malls to being review sites (which are hard to monetize), to being blogs which may offer a bit of both and more. Here are a few unique models to learn from.

ZampleBox, Seattle, WA (www.ZampleBox.com)

Tony Mandarano was a born entrepreneur. He watched his father build a community of fans of expensive Italian sports cars and much of what his dad did subconsciously sunk in. While in college Tony started smoking but shortly after decided to quit, which was challenging. He was introduced to vaping in 2009 and saw quickly the "Big Picture." What is the Big Picture? This industry, this product, is the most *revolutionary paradigm* shift we have seen in decades. That is my description, not his, but Tony sees that as well. Tony's question to himself was "What does this mean to the entire world?" which is a terrific "Big Picture" question to ask of yourself. There have been millions of smokers that have tried to quit, most unsuccessfully. Can vaping and e-cigs shift those percentages to the positive side?

Prior to his exposure to vaping and seeing the potential, Tony was heading down another road, the tech road. He was computer and programming savvy and was interested in pursuing those avenues before focusing on vaping. As he investigated the market he saw more potential, less competition and, just as important, an industry where he could leave an impact. So what did he do? He dug in and Tony, at age 24, understood how technology could take this product into the hands of anyone with a computer. Rather than go the more "traditional routes," Tony decided he did not want to "just" do a store, nor did he want to create a review site which was difficult to monetize.

Starting very simply he bought starter kits at wholesale prices and developed a web site to sell them. This was fine for his college years but as his proficiency grew it was time to look beyond the obvious and find a unique business model, which is every entrepreneur's dream. He was scared away for a while by the FDA's battle with NJOY and the potential demise of the industry but he continued to monitor the progress until he had a sense of a future.

In September 2013 he had the epiphany of developing a subscription based program that people buy into and get top quality e-liquid that has already been screened with some assurance of high quality. Each month a sample box (or ZampleBox) is delivered to their mailbox and though that sounds simple in concept it is technologically challenging. Every month they need to do the reviewing and develop new SKU numbers for each product, get them mailed out and basically provide service at the highest level.

Now after one year Tony has a team and a following of strong advocates. I was introduced to him by one of those fans at a vaping event in Salt Lake City. The owner of a Vape shop showed me a sample and gushed over their services, so she got my attention and I reached out to Tony to dig into the back story.

What did Tony do right and where did he go askew?

The answers may be too hard to determine since the company is just one year old. Generally the first year success rate of most businesses is very high but drops precipitously after that and the failure rate after five years is about 90%; it may be higher in this Vape Space. From what I see ZampleBox has grown slowly, and did it with good strategy and commendable execution. Whether they are profitable or not is not the question here, but are they providing something that people want? Is there a pain they are fixing, a need they are filling? For now that would be a "yes," and time will tell if this is a sustainable model.

VapeFinds, Los Angeles, CA (www.VapeFinds.com)

If there is one underlying theme with all these entrepreneurs that word is PASSION. They all have a passion for the *cause* and the ability to deliver an alternative and healthier smoking device. With some they go the traditional store; for others, especially those with tech skills, maybe a web store is the easiest first step. If someone comes from a background of manufacturing or science, then building a better mousetrap, or in this case, a better mod or component or e-liquid may be a more natural step.

But what if you want to get a handle on the industry itself? The question has been asked by many, "How many Vape shops are there in the country?" and the truth is, no one knew. Actually no one had any ideas or just guessed, but now we have some data to refer to.

When I entered the market in July 2013 I asked that question of everyone that I thought could answer. I inquired of CASAA and SFATA and every organized group I could find, but found nothing. So I started keeping a database myself and developing my own records.

At the Vapetoberfest in Long Beach in 2013 fortune brought Jeff Huyen and me together. I was chatting with someone about the lack of data, he introduced me to Jeff who addressed my questions with his online directory of Vape stores nationwide. At the time he had about 2000, but by summer 2014, that number has tripled and VapeFinds has one of the most complete databases of anyone in the country.

The goal of VapeFinds is to enable anyone looking for a shop to find them in any city in the country. Do you have a favorite juice? Type it into their app and find a Vape shop that carries it. No more random searches in stores that offer no solution. This application is free to the consumer and free to the customer. Stores can input the data of their changing inventory in real time which relieves VapeFinds of the responsibility.

Jeff validated some of the results that I found about the number of stores starting as well as those closing.

When I asked the question of "How do you make money?" the response was that they intend to be the "Google of the vaping industry." What does that mean??

Many search engines, merchant providers and other databases do not like or respect this industry and we run into problems with Pay Pal, E-bay and other processing gateways. Google doesn't want our ad revenue, nor do Facebook and others. Jeff's plan is to have a comprehensive database of any and all related industries, from brick and mortar stores to merchant services to accessories, supplies, etc… When you build the traffic, revenue will come and his model is working and growing in size and monetizing more every month. In time Google and the others will take note and lighten up.

As I finished my conversation with Jeff I came around to the question that started this whole chase: How many stores do we have in the United States?

His answer: "Brick & Mortar stores, about 5,000-6,000, and adding in hybrid stores including convenience stores, smoke shops, the Costco and Wal-marts of the world and we're looking at 20,000-35,000 stores."

I also asked where the "hot spots" in the country were and he picked "California, Texas, Florida, and Arizona and New York tied for #4, in that order." Surprisingly Minnesota is a strong player with 200 stores added in just the past few months.

What did Jeff and VapeFinds do right and where did he falter?:

- Jeff and his crew have been at every event I have attended in 2014, from Chicago to Las Vegas to Miami and that is a great way to make yourself significant.
- They "play with everyone" which means that much of the infighting that I see with many factions in this industry they do not follow. He has competitors but they bash no one.
- Their attitude of the company is "***innovate don't imitate***" and that is a great mindset with his entire team.
- So far I have seen few missteps and see many new projects and opportunities coming their way. I commend their willingness to learn and to teach.

Other components & products

There are many successful businesses that have monetized the Vape Space in different ways. Brandon Nelson started

Kryptonite Tanks in 2013 and has carved out a very strong presence in the marketplace and is doing terrific. Here's how he got started:

Kryptonite Tanks, Santa Ana, CA (www.KryptoniteTanks.com)

Brandon Nelson had a very successful mortgage business for fourteen years and like many had to make adjustments in the aftermath of 2008. After that he started working for a friend and helped him to market and rebuild that company. It wasn't his passion but he had the skills and grew that company three fold in less than two years then looked for what he really wanted to pursue, which was manufacturing.

I have visited many Vape shops in Southern California and most of them carried this interesting line of products called Kryptonite Tanks. With their recognizable neon green displays they stood out and when I ran into the owner several months ago we exchanged cards and wanted to dig into his story to share with you.

Brandon's family background was in engineering and in manufacturing and with a friend in the vape industry found some opportunities in representing new products after he left his previous position. He offered different products and saw a need in something that many take for granted: vaping tanks. Like many solopreneurs he decided to venture out on his own rather than partner with anyone. Initially carto tanks were the norm and Brandon found out what people liked and what they didn't. After many surveys he noted that most wanted to buy American, but they were cost prohibitive. Chinese products were cheaper, but they had a short lifespan. He looked at different materials and found harder materials and glass that were all US made and started Kryptonite Tanks in September of 2013. He now has several different locations that specialize in different components and he assembles everything in Southern California. A point to note: this fit perfectly into Brandon's background since he knew manufacturing and engineering while many others would be overwhelmed.

In years past when an entrepreneur had an idea like this they would open a machine shop, get all the equipment and materials and do everything in house. That model is not as effective for smaller runs and may be a direction that Brandon may choose to follow in the future, but for the time being it makes more sense to outsource everything.

Kryptonite is strictly a manufacturer and does no retail sales and is approaching their first anniversary. I asked Brandon, as an experienced entrepreneur, what he did right, what he wished he had done differently and what he had learned. His responses:

- He should have brought some of his products out sooner because the market moves so quickly and the costumer wants new and innovative **now**.
- He is very busy and in many cases takes on too much, which can limit bandwidth and delivery times.
- He stuck with the brand and made sure it was *right,* which delivered a top quality product. In most cases

- patience and quality control will give you an edge over your competition even if it takes a bit more time.
- His initial revenue projections were met and his business is growing substantially. His company delivers worldwide with several different lines and sells thousands of products monthly.
- Closing words to someone that wants "in" to the Vape Space but does not want to go the conventional retail/e-liquid, online way: "Don't go into anything unless you commit to innovating and not just remodeling." He echoes the words of Jeff with VapeFinds in that this market is *ripe* for innovators and will recognize imitators very quickly.

I know many others that are craftsmen and create beautiful (and expensive) glass tips. VapeSox created sleeves for holding your pens and e-liquid and batteries and a host of other "things" you need to carry and don't have enough pocket room for them.

One of the more challenging problems that new Vape shop owners find is dependable and affordable supplies, including e-liquid and hardware. At one time both were difficult and finding good e-liquid, one that is manufactured to high standards with great taste, was not easy. Today great quality e-liquids with high purity made in a **clean room** are everywhere. The media concerns of "where did it come from?" and "was it made in someone's bathtub?" is less common than years past. These were just fodder for media hype and hysteria.

Many have started e-liquid companies or added the manufacturing or wholesaling to supply their own stores. These stories will be shared in "Masters of Vapes," my new book, due in 2015.

Are there other niches that can be filled by ingenious entrepreneurs?

Right now we're just asking the questions and shortly will share some of the answers.

VAPESOX

VapeSox, Brea, CA (www.VapeSox.com)

Can you make money in the Vape Space with accessories and add-ons? Becky and Greg Miron launched VapeSox in September 2013, first by testing it in a local store and then going big by going to Las Vegas VapeFest with just 100 units. They sold out quickly and wished they had taken more.

Becky just crested age 50 and does not normally consider herself an entrepreneur. But her son was. Becky actually worked—and continues to work—for a fiber optics company where she has been for 30 years and in addition was a smoker for 35 years. She was introduced to vaping by her son who created a pouch to contain his hardware and bottles. Becky told her son he should just "go buy one" and he responded by stating, "There is nothing out there like this," and a vision was born. **Point #1**. Look for holes in the market place and see if you can fill it.

Becky and her family worked together on the designs and continue to work together as a true family business. With most of them involved in the day to day operation of the business, she and her husband Greg brought some experience and a bit of the reality check. Gregg had a background in operations which is a great foundation and he has been a big part of their growth.

A point to note is that her products are U.S. made in Orange County, California, which we all want to see and respect if it makes economic sense and for now they have no interest in overseas production. She remains on her job but sees the day when she will need to work VapeSox full time. **Point #2**. It's great to go "all in" but unless you have financial reserve or additional forms of income, keep your jobs as long as you need to.

One of the things we talked about is "Value Proposition" which she has used in her career for three decades and taught her sons to honor as well. What's *your* value? WHY should your customers buy from you? The adage of "If you build it they will come" is not true and unless you provide value, you will never go or stay big. **Point #3**.

I asked about sales and volume and Becky shared that from month one, just 13 months earlier, they have experienced monthly growth of 25% which is a huge acceleration curve that will eventually slow down but a great way to launch and get traction. They see knockoffs and imitators every day so remain watchful of illegal competition. One way to avoid that, in addition to creating value, is by offering variety which they do with 65+ SKUs for every combination anyone would want. **Point #4**: variety, selection and personalization.

Their biggest challenge today is managing growth, which is a wonderful problem to have! When I asked for any closing words, she shared: "If you have an idea, but don't know what you're doing, find someone to help you, whether it be a friend or a mentor, but DO NOT give up on your dream. You DO NOT need to be stuck in a boring job and if you truly believe in what you are doing, just do it with focus." We'll call that **Point #5.**

Becky and her VapeSox crew and I have crossed paths many times in just the short time we have both been in the business, and they always have crowds at their booths since they do offer a unique product. I wanted to include her profile to accentuate that anyone, at any age, of any sex, can create a successful business in the vaping industry.

AFFILIATE PROGRAMS

These can take many different forms and could be as simple as developing your own e-liquid review site or tapping into heavy web traffic on your site that may or may not be related to this industry. Affiliate programs are huge and have the potential of being the largest revenue generator available. Here's an example and also a brief introduction to one of my heroes, John Lee Dumas, who started a podcast called **"Entrepreneur on Fire.**" He is not in the Vape Space but has become a legend in developing Affiliate revenue.

His goal was to do a daily, 365 day podcast and interview successful entrepreneurs. He had zero experience and everyone, including "experts," told him it could not be done. "Not enough time." "Not enough people to interview." "You'll never be able to monetize it." Those objections would deter most people but John knew it could be done and he knew he could do it.

Since launching in September 2012 John has interviewed almost 800 entrepreneurs including the very famous, like Brian Tracy, Seth Godin, to the ones that were not well known, myself included (#467). His podcast is ranked at the top on every platform and he has close to one million monthly downloads. He also is making a ton of money.

John records all his shows in one day, Monday, then spends the week marketing and editing. His small team is generating over $200,000 monthly income and his net is about 75% of that. Much of his income is affiliate programs of any and all sorts and that is passive residual income. They told him it could not be done, told him it was never done before. He proved them wrong and you can prove any of your critics wrong as well. You need passion, a plan, guidance, execution and a bit of luck.

Can YOU develop your own Affiliate network?? If you get web traffic or have the ability to get web traffic, you absolutely can monetize this channel. ZazzleBox and VapeFinds are two of the best examples of those that are adding Affiliate programs to their business model since they get lots of traffic and are building a loyal following.

E-LIQUID (JUICE) MANUFACTURING

How awesome is that, your own line of juice! John's juice? Ass-kicking Vape juice! You can name it what you want but there are huge caveats here and most people that develop their own line of juice do it wrong. For the sake of elevating our vocabulary (and with thanks to Maria Verven's suggestion) we will call juice by the more official name, "**e-liquid**." The street name will always be juice but when it comes to manufacturing and legislation that is the name generally used.

Point #1: this is not a project to be taken lightly and getting reputable e-liquid from a reputable company is paramount. ***Do not*** make it yourself or buy from a "friend" making it at home. We (as an industry) have been incredibly lucky since no one has died or gotten horribly sick with contaminated product. Even though there are just a few ingredients, any one of them could be a source of contamination or improper mixing method and if someone gets sick or worse you know who's all over this? CNN. FOX News. All the major newspapers, since this is a *good story*, but horrible PR.

Point #2

There is *no* reason to have your own line until you have a brand established and a following, otherwise this is just an ego play and costs you money and time and is distracting. When you have a location or online store and have a loyal following and reputation then maybe your own line is a good idea. And do not create flavors on the fly or on a whim. Find out what your customers want and reverse engineer it.

Sometimes starting with e-liquid production opens up other opportunities and in many cases successful Vapreneurs have bypassed the typical e-liquid production line to develop or import the hardware, a more cumbersome process.

In the past year I have seen more e-liquid manufacturers pop up than almost any other model besides brick & mortar stores. Some of these are not *true* manufacturers since they sometimes "white label" or "private label" someone else's products. That is perfectly fine but it is important to put YOUR brand or mark on YOUR products if you want this idea to grow.

Usually the best way to start is to find out what **your** clients and customers want. Are they big into the fruit flavors? The candies? Menthol lines? Liquor flavoring? This is not a decision to take on lightly and you always want to sell what people want, not offer what you have.

If you do decide to follow this path it is a serious commitment of time and especially money since you will need to commit to minimum runs of several hundred to several thousand bottles per month. What size is best? What shape bottle? Those are your choices and you get those answers by testing the market.

How much does it cost to launch a business like this? Should I sell at flea markets or swap meets? Should I get ingredients from China?

Now of these are to be taken lightly and we have been providing guidance in these areas for a long time.

MadVapes, Mooresville, NC (www.MadVapes.com)

Mark Hoogendoorn didn't start out as a manufacturer of juice and had a pretty inauspicious beginning selling hardware and some product from the trunk of his car and from his garage. From that beginning in 2009 MadVapes is now one of the major players in the e-liquid market. Like many, Mark's motivation came from his desire to quit smoking and the lack of success using conventional patches and gum. He bought his first mod on E-bay in a spur of the moment decision, and after it broke much too quickly he realized that there was a need, a pain that he could fill.

A tinkerer by passion with an IT background, he tried to create mods and devices based on common sense and gradually increased his knowledge to the point of pulling out a $10,000 loan from his retirement account. Commitment like that is required to really create a difference and soon he was outgrowing his garage and his house and needed more and larger facilities.

A Baby Boomer like myself since Mark is 51, he typifies what we see in this industry and that is, entree by experienced, sophisticated entrepreneurs. This is a paradigm shift from what has been the "norm" from the beginning and is a definite sign of the future. Those characteristics allowed the company to grow to 22 brick and mortar locations, primarily in the mid-Atlantic area, but soon expanding beyond. A neighbor, Scott Church, was a chef who soon discovered he had a knack for creation of e-liquids in addition to his food repertoire and soon he was on board.

MadVapes has 50 flavors that are very popular with a total listing of more than 200 choices. Traditional flavors seems to sell, like banana or blueberry, but menthols remain one of the top sellers. As other manufacturers have shared, the "candy flavors" are not big sellers and the media's charge against "appealing to children" is mostly unfounded.

When asked about the direction or trends towards nicotine strength, Mike Schrieffer, marketing VP at MadVapes, shares that nicotine variety ranges across the spectrum, though the direction seems to be leading towards lower or even no nicotine levels. We have seen the same thing in Southern California.

As prominent as MadVapes is in the e-liquid market, they are currently the largest retail brick and mortar sellers in the country. In the Charlotte, NC area they have eight stores and remote locations that range from Boston to New Jersey, to Atlanta and west into Texas and soon a flagship location on the west coast. They are not a franchise, but instead operate under a licensing agreement and plan to double their numbers by the end of 2015

Chapter FIVE: What's your story?

The goal of this book is to provide an overall viewpoint and perspective of the Vape Space as a business. It is a snapshot, a moment in time, in this very dynamic industry and offered to provide a perspective of where this industry has been, where it is now and where it may be going. The question of whether **you** fit in is your choice, but my passion is supporting, nurturing and growing entrepreneurs. Hell, it's the only world I've known for forty years and I have made enough mistakes for all of you. So learn from me; let me teach you. Let's start here.

I shared earlier that I walked into my first Vape Shop in Newport Beach, California on the 4th of July 2013. Independence Day is without a doubt the wildest day of the year in this seaside party town. After finishing an event for the newspaper I write for I went to the beach to check out the craziness. Walking by a Vape Shop (which I did not recognize) I did a double-take, walked back in and asked the question that changed my world forever: "**What the Hell is a Vape Shop?**"

That started a whole series of events including doing lots of research, studying the history of this fledgling industry and seeing the potential along with many, many chances to carve a niche.

As a restless entrepreneur since my twenties, I made a horrible employee. I questioned everything and saw ways to do things "better" at least in my naïve mind. At age 26 I started in real estate, had lots of drive and energy and motivation but certainly no experience nor guidance or leadership. Add in circumstances that were **outside** my control like a crappy market and a Prime Rate that hit 20.5%

as I got into the industry and that made selling homes "challenging."

Creativity became the only way to survive, which I did for many years but I lost my passion very quickly and felt limited in my ability to expand and grow and scale. This was the eighties, pre-internet, and pre-technology, just barely the beginning of the computer and PC age. In the early 90's I started one of the first pre-foreclosure and short sale businesses in California and did well but foolishly walked away when I could have extended it much longer. I had an over inflated ego, which has been the undoing of many, including me.

I met a very successful entrepreneur that did many things I always wanted to do, including speaking on stage and training and teaching along with developing a company with national growth potential. After working with him for about a year I saw signs of trouble as his tolerance for risk crossed the line and I left before things got worse. They did and after I left he went to jail. Lesson learned. If you sense a sinking ship, change ships. Maturity takes time and is tough to rush.

A few years of exploration and trying to regain PASSION and eventually I stumbled across the mortgage industry. I embraced it with a vengeance and did exceedingly well and later opened my own mortgage business in 2002. By "coincidence" though I no longer believe in randomness anymore, I was offered an opportunity to be part of a radio show that had an extraordinary audience but a host that knew nothing about real estate or mortgages. My "Mortgage Minute" made me a lot of money and this time timing was on my side as the market heated up. By the following year I took a huge leap and started my own radio show with a friend that complemented my skills and personality. He was the "straight man" and I was the "wacky sidekick" but "The Real Estate and Finance Show with Norm and Mike" was a success for many years. We developing a great following, did many live workshops, taught thousands of listeners how to invest and what to do and what NOT to do. This was all part of a process of growth and even through it all I was lacking in something that I sorely regret. Mentorship.

The year 2008 devastated my world along with most of my income and net worth. My marriage soon was caught in that wake and at age 54 I had no idea what I was going to do as a 30 year career was virtually wiped out in one calendar quarter.

Later I developed a business acceleration program for entrepreneurs and worked with SCORE, the SBA, cities and chambers and consulted with hundreds of different businesses that were stuck, as I had been. I learned that most everything that worked prior to 2008 stopped working and this New Age was very difficult for many, including myself.

Fast forward a few years to the pivotal 2013 when I left a house, a wife, a life and partnership that I held for many years and totally got Spiritual and stopped trying to control everyone and everything in my life. I listened and paid attention more than I ever had and thankfully, in those 2008-2012 years I was blessed with a business partner that was also a mentor. I was late to that empowerment party but I know that I saved lots of time and failures by having his guidance.

I consider myself a pro at Reinvention since I did it many times over a 40 year career. My entrepreneurial spirit was uncontrollable at times and I was a loose cannon. When I reinvented myself one more time in the Vape Space I knew I wanted to help budding entrepreneurs avoid many of the failures I experienced along with others I knew. There is more to the story and if you Google my name you can listen to several podcasts I did as a *guest*, not a host, where I share my story, failures and success.

If I look back on my life and all the skills I have learned, my passion for vaping is not an accident. Since I wrote and published a book on Baby Boomers, Millennials and mentoring, called "Success at Any Age: The Baby Boomer's and Gen Y's Guide to becoming an Overnight Success," along with writing many articles, it was a natural transition to write for Vape News Magazine. My love of radio and broadcasting made Vape News Radio an easy add-on. Public speaking and training has been in my blood since 1981 when I joined Toastmasters, so doing presentations in front of one or one thousand doesn't faze me.

Nothing happens by accident—including YOU reading this book. How or if you act is within your control but I suggest you pay attention to "random" events in your life since they rarely are...

Over the past year I have written many Special Reports which are listed below:

- Starting, Growing, Branding and Maximizing your Vape Store Potential"
- "Top SEVEN questions to ask before you open your Vape store"
- "FIVE ways to dominate your Vapor market"
- How e-cigs and the Vape movement will repair the tarnished image of Big Tobacco

- The Missing Ingredient in the Vape Space: Customer Service
- How much does it COST to open a Vape Shop?
- Lung Cancer Decreases as Vaping Increases"--A dialogue that engaged...
- How to open a Vape Store when you have No Money
- Tapping into your "Natural" market
- The Criminalization of Vaping
- The Reinvention of Smoke Shops
- So What Exactly IS a Lounge?
- The Healthier side of Vaping
- The Vaping Bubble:
- The FDA Decision: What it really means
- The-Vaping-Trend-early-adapters-demographics

By the time you read this there may be more. I was tempted to reproduce them all here but would rather you look at them at your own pace and not lose whatever momentum you have to continue on.

They can be viewed at:
http://vapementors.com/special-reports/

We also have over three dozen radio show segments from Vape New Radio. The show is comprised of three parts. Part I usually brings you up to date on current events in legislation or regulation, along with event and fests and things you should know. Parts II and II typically involve interviews with some of the Movers & Shakers in this industry.

They can be heard at: http://VapeNewsRadio.com.

You can also subscribe at ITunes:

https://itunes.apple.com/us/podcast/vape-news-radio/id900238570

Or Stitcher directory for Android users:

http://www.stitcher.com/podcast/vape-news-radio

We also **video** the radio show and post them on YouTube if you'd like to check that out, too.

Vape News Radio started on April 21, 2014 and as this final edit is completed we are proud to see our downloads break the 180,000 mark with over 35,000 each month, with a worldwide audience in over 30 countries. **Thank you all**.

As an aside and to highlight the challenges of this business:

The Vape Shop I first walked into was originally called Newport Vapor Shop. Believe it or not they were threatened with a lawsuit by Newport BRAND tobacco (Lorillard) and changed their name to 32nd Street Vape Shop.

That shop never quite found its mark and was a poignant example of a great location and great potential and poor execution. It was due to an owner that let ego blind him (more on that later) and recently that shop was SOLD to a friend that owns one of the most successful e-liquid companies around. I have no doubt that this store will be brought to its former and unrealized glory.

Let's get back on track with Vapreneur and your goals and intentions.

We'll now be taking a little side trip about you and how to identify your strengths and weaknesses. It may seem a distraction, but understanding these things is critical in pursuing your journey.

After you read through the following we'll finish with your roadmap. The roadmap is very flexible and will be personalized to you. It will incorporate much of what these special reports cover as well as the next sets of exercises so I recommend you not gloss over them but read them all. Make and take notes. ANY information you find helpful write it down. Keep a notebook and when you are done you'll have enough information to get you started. You can then make adjustments to your current business to advance to the next step.

Chapter SIX: The "Personal Development" side of business and entrepreneurship.

Before we get into specific steps to understanding the Vaping industry and where you fit in—and IF you fit in—we need to start with the person behind the business. I have said for years that most businesses do not fail because of a bad **business**, they usually fail because of a bad **owner**. EGO has killed more businesses than any "bad economy" and I have seen this first hand multiple times over the years. There are many, many ways to screw up a business or do it wrong and just a few ways to do it well.

We all have our skills and our weaknesses which I discuss throughout many of the Special Reports, but many times we really don't understand ourselves beyond that and for this example we're talking about the words "**Competence**" and "**Incompetence**."

Do not take offense at those words because saying you are incompetent at something does not imply anything bad or derogatory. For me personally I know what I am good at and I know the very many things that I am not good at. Case in point:

- Do not give me a big spreadsheet to review or analyze. If it fits on one page that is awesome! If I have to scroll down and reference different tables and cells, you've lost me.
- I hate reviewing legal contracts or complex laws. I spent decades in real estate and financial services and read many contracts and complex forms. Usually after about three pages my attention span has left me. I'm a simple guy and speak with simple language. Even reading the reports that come out of CASAA

and SFATA I boil down into the basics since I understand that many of you reading this do not have the time or interest in reading every nuance of everything we need to know.

While writing this book my goal was to tell the stories we can all relate to in simple and pure terms. I wanted to keep it short enough so you will have greater insight to your business as well as yourself.

Back to the Four Levels which have been shared in a very simple theory called "*The Four Levels of Competence*."

The four 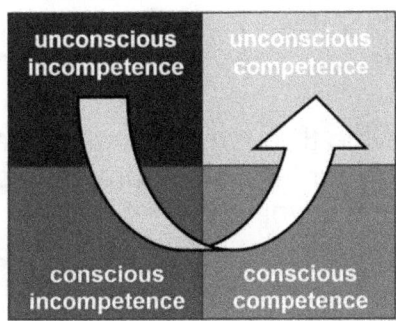 **stages**

1. **Unconscious incompetence**

    This is an example of "you don't know what you don't know." This is where we start everything in our lives, from learning to talk and walk and read and write, and then getting into more specific skills. We act and do impulsively and based on instinct which may be right and adequate and sometimes not.

    In the world of vaping this is where many used to start but less now than before. Not too long ago there *were* no rules and guidelines and it truly was a vacant landscape. Could you do things improperly and still "succeed?" The answer **was** "yes," but that is becoming less common. Since many were young and inexperienced the first level is where many started—and remain.

Before you move on to Stage Two, you must realize and recognize what you ***don't know*** and that is called…

2. **Conscious incompetence**

    Now you realize where you are missing key components. You want to learn math but you didn't memorize your multiplication table. You want to be a better driver but after a few tickets maybe you finally understand that you need to go back to basics.

    Instead of moving through a cloud you see deficiencies in your life or in your business model. The cure for that is you either:
    a) Learn how to do it yourself
    b) Have someone teach you how to do it
    c) Find someone else to do it

    When you recognize what you didn't know before you move into Stage Three which is where the huge majority of business owners reside.

3. **Conscious competence**

    You know what to do and you do it. It usually comes easily but you may have mini "aha" moments that make you aware of the things you need to do.

    Someone comes into your shop and asks a question. You pause for a moment, dig into your memory banks or skill sets, and come up with an answer. You *know* the answer but had to regroup internally to come up with it.

Some people live in this world most of their lives. They don't quite assimilate things internally but must pause for that moment before responding. When you are truly proficient at what you do you move into the level that we all aspire to:

4. **Unconscious competence**

    A perfect example is driving a car. **You do things automatically without giving it much thought.** You check the windows and mirrors, monitor your speed and braking and get from Point A to Point B many times without even being conscious of the trip. The ride to and from work is like this many times. You're on the phone, listening to the radio or music and before you know it you're at your destination.

    Many of us become Unconsciously Competent at many things in our lives. If we have played sports and became proficient you know that most of your reactions became subconscious. In baseball when you are at bat and the pitcher throws a ball, we usually get proficient enough that we recognize the good pitches from the bad. Off the field and in business, when someone asks you a question about something you really, truly understand you reply without hesitation.

    A customer comes in with a mod that they need help with and it's a question you have heard many times. You don't think about the response you just ACT. It's second nature; it's automatic. This response comes out of either passion for a particular subject or experience with it.

THIS is where you want to be in your business. And do not think you have to have **all** the answers at your fingertips. No one person can be the master of everything, but a **true** master knows how to find answers. You either find a teacher or hire someone that does.

I'm a fan of comics and some cartoons and thought this timely:

Easter Egg #2: What is the ultimate last stage of the Four Stages of Competence?

You may be asking yourself, "**WHY is all this stuff necessary?**" The answer is easy: Businesses do not fail; people do.

What that means is that if you are serious about getting into this industry—or any industry—it is up to YOU to succeed or fail. And one of the biggest reasons that I have seen that causes a business to fail:

ego

(Reference my initial visit to my first Vape Shop) We could spend a lot of time on the psychology of the ego and why sometimes it is called "The Inner Asshole," but I share below this easy pictorial of what determines if one mind is coachable and geared for success, or if another is "closed off" and may (not always) fail.

As a business coach one of the questions I ask my clients is "Are you coachable?" Some say no, most say yes, and most of those really *are* but the rest are deluding themselves. Some want validation of their own thoughts and directions and are closed off to outside suggestions. They *think* they are coachable, but they are "emotionally attached to their own bad ideas," as my former business partner and mentor used to claim. And it's true.

Change **will** happen and you should embrace it. You should not "get attached to outcomes" but put pieces in place to create the outcome you wish.

One of my business associates felt he got burned in a business transaction. He was angry and felt the fool and thought he was taken advantage off and he shared with me the following:

He said I am NOT in the business to make friends. So I responded, "No you're not, but it helps." I advised him to be *friendly* with everyone but not concerned with making friends.

WHY are you in business? We all have different reasons. When the WHY is clear enough and big enough, the hows will emerge.

I believe you can make friends, make money, make a difference and leave a legacy if you have the right mindset.

In the graphic below you can identify where you stand on the "coachability" scale. Are you open to new ideas or do you want your current ideas validated?

Will your ego keep you locked into where you are or free you into someone else?

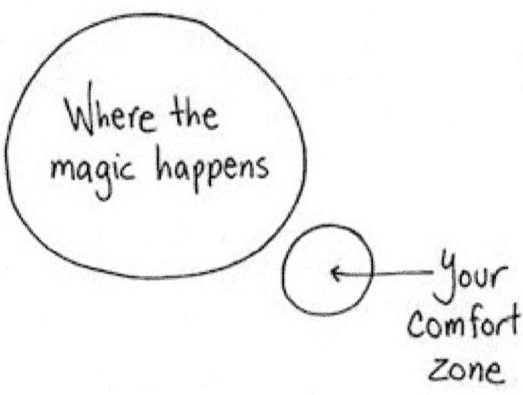

TWO MINDSETS
CAROL S. DWECK, Ph.D.
Graphic by Nigel Holmes

Fixed Mindset
Intelligence is static

Leads to a desire to look smart and therefore a tendency to...

Growth Mindset
Intelligence can be developed

Leads to a desire to learn and therefore a tendency to...

CHALLENGES
...avoid challenges
...embrace challenges

OBSTACLES
...give up easily
...persist in the face of setbacks

EFFORT
...see effort as fruitless or worse
...see effort as the path to mastery

CRITICISM
...ignore useful negative feedback
...learn from criticism

SUCCESS OF OTHERS
...feel threatened by the success of others
...find lessons and inspiration in the success of others

As a result, they may plateau early and achieve less than their full potential.

All this confirms a **deterministic view of the world.**

As a result, they reach ever-higher levels of achievement.

All this gives them a **greater sense of free will.**

Chapter SEVEN: Creating your future in the Vape Space

Let's build a Strategy:

Step one:

- Identify your interests in this industry.
- Identify your skills sets and ways to monetize them.

Step two:

- Discover the biggest needs or pains you think exist in the Vape Space.
- What skills do you have to resolve some of them?

Step three:

- Who (if anyone) do you need—or have—to execute some type of plan? Yes, you can start alone but one saying I live with is, "You can fail by yourself, but you cannot succeed alone."
- What complementary or supplementary skills do they bring to your vision?

Step four:

- For you to execute your dream, what capital do you need?
- Do you have it, and if not, how can you find it?

Step five:

- You've identified the needs, your skills, your team and your budget. Identify (in writing) how you execute and when.

- What obstacles may stop you that may *appear* to be deal killers?
- What is your "brand?," and understand that it is **more** than just a logo…

Let's put together a process and system

By this point you've put a very rough framework together of your business model. How do you execute??

Before we get into that let's address the question of Business Planning or more specifically, creating a Business Plan.

A Business Plan is the foundation, the formulation of almost every notable business in existence. No business can be formed and grow and dominate by operating without one. We may start by flying blind, but you cannot remain there and if you need capital it is a requirement.

I have been involved in the world of business planning for many years. The Small Business Administration (SBA) is one of the best resources to help "small business," usually identified as those with fewer than 500 employees. It started officially in 1953, but really began decades earlier as a directive by President Herbert Hoover as the Great Depression was still mired in stagnation. They are notable on many levels, but primarily as being the Guarantor of Small Business Loans. Understand that the SBA is **not** a lender, but they guarantee loans that are generated by banks that are approved to do so.

The SBA is very conservative and traditional and highly bureaucratic. I have been involved with them for many years and have offered many training programs under their directions and guidelines as well as one of their sub-organizations called SCORE. SCORE used to stand for "Service Corp of Retired Executives" when it started in 1964 and was primarily a place for retired professionals and executives to help teach and mentor younger ones.

Like everything else, this organization has changed over the years and now many of the SCORE volunteers are younger, more entrepreneurial and female. In 2008 as my 30 year career was coming to an end I started working with SCORE as a mentor and conducted many trainings and classes. It was a great experience and the persons that go to SCORE for counseling get decades' worth of experience for free.

Both SBA and SCORE are huge proponents of business plans and spend lots of energy and time to help develop, formulate and implement on behalf of the business community. Their primary focus is to help the business owner develop a plan to get an SBA loan which many do since NO bank will ever finance any business without a business plan. They are very specific and very structured and can range from a small number of pages to an unwieldy number of pages. For sample templates visit www.SBA.gov or www.SCORE.org. Banks want easy to understand Business Plans and if what they see does not meet their requirements at a very quick read, it most likely will be rejected.

What does this have to do with *our* business, the Vape Space? Will a bank do an SBA loan for a new start up store? The answer is "doubtful." I have never seen one, I have seen hundreds ask and dozens try and since banks are notoriously risk averse and this business is highly risky, I do not expect to see one anytime soon.

Does that mean loans are not available and you do not need a Business Plan?

If a loan is to be obtained it will probably be a secured real estate loan or a personal loan based on good credit and good income. CAVEAT: If you are seeking a loan for a vaping business I suggest you *not* say that. Don't lie, but be discreet about your intentions.

When I am asked about Business Plans, my response is that "I am a fan of Business Plans, but not an advocate."

Should you create a Business plan for **you**? I say yes, though it need not be as comprehensive as many templates that are available through SBA or SCORE. Since most aspiring business owners do a Business Plan for the purpose of borrowing, and since that is probably not an option *here*, we developed a variation which I call a **Business Modeling Template**. It is very specific in its' focus and is devoid of most financial projections. Why is that? Primarily because there *are* no formats or pro-formas for this industry that are available. We have been collecting them at VapeMentors and will be sharing those in future updates, but for now it is more guesswork than history.

Here is a condensed version which can help you get started on your Business Model.

This is not a conventional business plan template. This is specific towards understanding certain key concepts:

1. your Customer
2. your Marketing Plan
3. your Competition
4. the "Market"
5. your Vision

Questions to be raised:

1. Strategy: What specific strategy or strategies would be most effective and personal to US as well as our targeted client/ audience?

2. Tactical concepts: more deep and long range. Where is this market going? Is there anything we can do to stay AHEAD of the wave and not be caught up in any adverse outcomes?

Part I: Find New Customers

Describe *your* customers, *their* problem(s), and how your product solves those problems. If you do not have a shop yet, use your best guess.

Product or service?

Do you believe you are supplying more of a product or a service? Define each and how they are different.

What are the problems or challenges your customers face?

How does your product/service solve their problems?

What is the biggest value your customers receive most when they buy from *you*?

Why do they make the decision to buy from *you*?

Describe your typical customer:

What "solutions" are they looking for?

How does what you offer help them?

What is the "typical" age and marital status of your customers?

What do you think your "average" customer "looks like?" Blue collar? White collar? Annual income?

Is there a predominant industry or profession they may be employed in?

Are there ethnic, racial, religious, or gender categories that you see or foresee as more dominant?

Any other identifiers of your "ideal" customer?

Part II: Your Marketing Plan

Do you have a:

- Company name
- Web site
- Logo
- Branding message

NOTE: DO NOT create them until you understand your basics and foundation.

WHAT IS?

Your "Message"?

Your marketing budget (monthly or annually)?

Your systems for implementation?

Will you be doing the marketing or use someone else?

Will you be doing the web site and SEO or use someone else?

Part III: Your Competition

How many similar stores are within 5 minutes/ 5 miles of your location? Double that?

Are there any that "dominate" the current market? How do you know??

What are the top three things you will do that is different/better than they?

1.
2.
3.

Part IV: The "market"

Where do YOU see "the market" going, both as an industry and based on regulations and legislation?

What do you see as a worst case scenario regarding the possible direction of the market?

How does YOUR CITY view vaping and Vape shops?

Do you understand how to "work" with the city regarding license, permits and dealing with city council or leaders?

How does YOUR STATE view vaping and Vape shops?

Part V: Your Vision

What do you see as your strategy over the next period of time?

6 months:

12 months:

18-24 months:

Anything beyond that is speculative, but think of terms for an exit strategy—even now. Do you see expansion beyond your current plan? Is this an entree to a different business or business model?

I highly suggest you dig into these questions either now or prior to making any specific steps into the Vape Space. All these questions are meaningful and important.

How to Proceed...

Based on the prior more detailed questionnaire, the following will allow you to put it in a condensed format.

Step one:

- Do you have or need a web site?
- What image of a logo or "brand" do you visualize?
- Strategize your online presence as to mechanics, logistics, flow, CRM (customer relationships management) and the specifics of how you execute.

Step two:

- Do you have the skills to create and execute those iconic images of your business?
- If you are developing an online shopping cart do you understand the processes to develop that?

Step three:

- If you plan on a brick & mortar location have you researched the position of your city regarding permits?
- Have you done any research on the competition?

Step four:

- Since we've addressed budgets before, do you know what is required to obtain a lease?
- Since you will (probably) need to do interior work before you open your doors, also called "tenant improvement" or TI, do you have any experience in knowing how best to execute that?
- Have you ever negotiated or obtained a commercial lease or know how to deal with real estate agents?
- Do you have any experience in hiring, teaching and training a staff?

Step five:

- A social media presence is not an option today, but a ***necessity***. Do you know the various channels, how to set up accounts and most important, how to use them properly?

- Aside from online media you should also know how to deal with "conventional" media, i.e., newspapers, radios and television. Have you done that before?

Step six:

- You need inventory, which means e-liquids and hardware. Do you know how to determine what is best and do you have relations and connections to get them?
- Determining WHAT to buy is critical, do you know how to research that subject?

An exercise in reality and common sense.

Below you is a picture of an airplane with all the various components identified. You've been in an airplane before and you probably never paid attention to them nor cared what they were called. What *did* you care about?

You wanted to get to your destination safely. You wanted to have fun or get done what you planned to do. All you want is the experience of getting to your final stop.

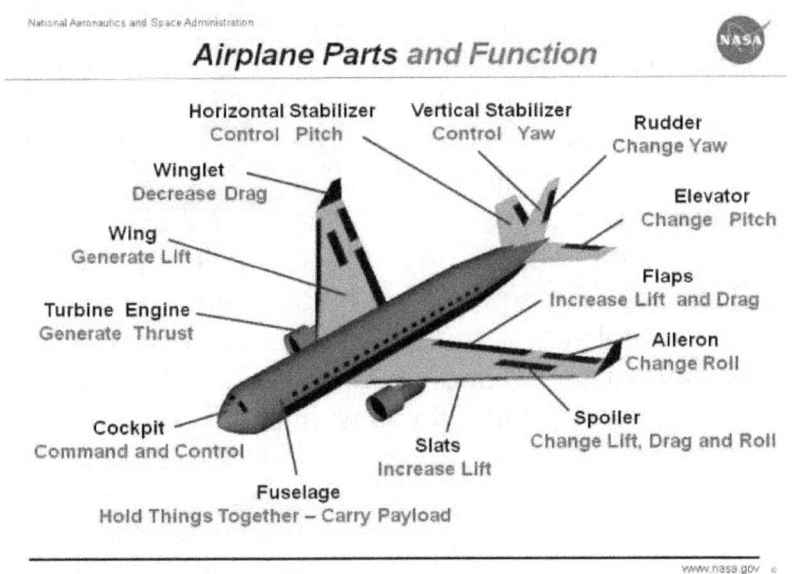

Compare that to vaping

Your customers generally don't care about the mechanical complexity or components of the vaping products they use. What do they care about?

They want flavor. They want comfort to hold it. They want to know this instrument will allow them to be tobacco or nicotine free. They want ease of you and to not be fearful.

They want to enjoy the experience and you must help them do that...

BEFORE YOU CONTINUE: SWOT

Danger Will Robinson: what TV show is this picture and saying from? (Easter Egg #3)

Many of you may be familiar with or have completed a SWOT Analysis. It is probably one of the *best* tools available for business owners in addition to the Business Plan and both these forms and concepts are not "one time things," but are ongoing. At one time you could create a Business Plan and it would be accurate and effective for several years. Today I suggest you review your plan (if you have one) and update your SWOT every six months or even every quarter if you want to stay on top of the rapid changes.

SWOT is an acronym which stands for **Strengths, Weaknesses, Opportunities and Threats** and is a quick snapshot of *your* business. From a gut reaction, take a few moments and think about your business OR the one you wish to create and address the following:

SWOT Analysis

Strengths 1 2 3 4 5	**Opportunities** 1 2 3 4 5
Weaknesses 1 2 3 4 5	**Threats** 1 2 3 4 5

Operation and processes improvements:
- How can your processes be made more seamless, fluid and easier to implement?

Training and personnel Improvements
- What's missing internally? Is your training process be as efficient and appropriate as possible?

Customer service, customer experiences:
- What are the improvements that can be implemented or changed to maximize the customer's positive experience?

Sales/ Marketing improvements (What is your message?)
- What easy to implement processes should be put in place to help you grow quickly, but under control?
- What easy and affordable processes can be implemented to grow rapidly?

Now what?:
1
2
3
4
5

Action Steps: what should be done first, quickly?

    Strengths
-

    Opportunities
-

Weaknesses
-

Threats
-

With unlimited funds we could/ should:

A SWOT analysis is vital and especially in our businesses due to the quick and frequent changes. New shop down the corner? Threat. One of our employees does something bad or stupid? Weakness. We get great press or social media buy in? Strength. New customer owns a business with lots of employees? Opportunity.

These situations, both good and bad can manifest very quickly and very frequently which is why a regular review is smart business.

Case study: why every shop is different

Every shop that opens is unique since they are a reflection of the owner, their experience, the location and competition and the surrounding market. Our thanks to Jon Brower, one of our clients that is now successfully running **Waldo Vapes** in Waldo, MO, a neighborhood of Kansas City, Mo. Jon has permitted us to share a bit of his Historiography, or history of his progress.

Jon is age 37, married and with a new child, just born, literally as his shop was also being created. His wife was his high school sweetheart and they were together for over 20 years when Jon decided he wanted to open his own shop. We started working together in spring 2014 and we'll highlight some of the steps involved in opening a shop and things to put into place long before you open your doors. Jon was not "testing" or trying a business, but was committed to doing this, so much that his wife quit her job so Jon could focus all his attention on fulfilling his dream.

Location: vitally important and Jon was fortunate that he found a great location with good foot traffic as well as drive-by. We were able to negotiate a 60 day ramp up period to do TI (tenant improvement) which was invaluable in generating buzz until we opened the end of June.

Kansas City and surroundings has a population of about 450,000 and Waldo had (when we started) several stores already open. His Vape Shop is situated in a strip center with five other businesses. Jon did his homework and observed that the public in his area did not like "chain stores" and preferred unique and even offbeat smaller businesses. With a unique name like "Waldo" we tapped into the "Where's Waldo?" children's book without stepping on anyone's toes and scheduled gatherings and meetings to be held at the shop even before we opened.

Jon was on top of his Social Media strategy and kept posting pictures along the lines of "coming soon" and included progress reports of the shop and the current condition as it came closer to readiness. People LOVE to be "involved" with the process and like to watch things as they unfold.

In the middle of June Jon had a "soft opening", which I recommend you do, followed by his Grand Event on June 21, which was an intentional date based on the longest day of the year. The response was universally positive with a great and overwhelming cry that he had a great line of e-liquids, which is one of the mainstays of the store.

First day's volume was modest but Jon proudly shared that for the first two weeks he sold to 100% of all those that entered the shop. Based on what he did the first day and the following week he was projecting to break the five figure mark, which he came very close to and missed by just a bit. Jon did this on his own with no employees which is sometimes the price we pay to be an entrepreneur and put in crazy long hours. His goal was to have adequate revenue for an employee and as he finished full month #2 he had one hired and on board for month #3. He also shared that he spent an inordinate amount of time with his customers, especially in the early days, and when we tracked that it was more than 1.5 hours per customer. Commitment.

One of his Competitive Positions is No Clones and the other is offering only the highest quality juice and already he has a reputation that backs that up. Employees from other Vape shops in town come to him for supply which says much about his competition and his astute palate.

Month #2 shattered the five figure mark as he broke through his daily averages every day for the first few weeks. As month three roles around Jon is well on his way to hitting the benchmark that I create for all our clients and that is $30K monthly revenue. When you hit that consistently for 60-90 days or more it is time to think about the "what's next" steps. Is it opening another location? Developing your own line of e-liquid? Everyone is different so you should revaluate your business model every calendar quarter to review what is working and what is not working.

As for Jon and Waldo Vape's expansion, his plan is location #2 identified or open by the end of 2014 and grow according to formula thereafter. More shops have opened in his area which does not concern Jon at all. He and I are in agreement in that "he has no competition," and if you also think like that it will afford you a greater peace of mind and less stress.

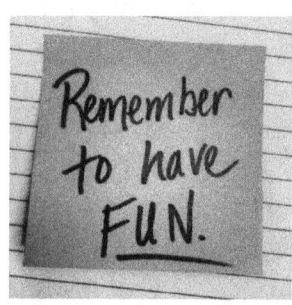

Let's make some money! The fun part: getting customers

You've developed your strategy and put in place systems and operational processes. The next question is, "**How do you get customers and how do you keep them??**" How do you create your own success story?

If you have done all that we have asked and completed these forms and asked specific questions, then we will leave that part up to you to figure out. You should be asking yourself these questions and many more and be sure you create your plan with FOCUS, with INTENTIONS and with expected or planned OUTCOMES. We can and will support and help you in this process. We normally advise you spend 50% of your time (initially) developing your strategy, 30% on developing systems and process and 20% on the gathering of customers. If you do the first two steps properly the last one will be easier.

Next steps?

Likewise, they are up to you. Are you a consumer and user of vaping products and find they've been helpful to control or eliminate your tobacco habits? Do you enjoy the freedom and money savings aspects? Regardless of the WHY, by all means continue to enjoy what you do.

We wish you luck on this New Journey.

Appendix:

A Historical Timeline of Electronic Cigarettes (a more expansive expose from page 4)

2003: The electronic cigarette is first developed in Beijing, China by **Hon Lik**, a 52 year old pharmacist, inventor and smoker. He reportedly invents the device after his father, also a heavy smoker, dies of lung cancer. The company Lik worked for, Golden Dragon Holdings, developed the device and changed their name to Ruyan, which means "like smoke." It should be noted that prior to Hon, the actual inventor of the 1st Ecig / smokeless cigarette was an American man named Herbert Gilbert, who patented the invention in 1963.

April 2006: Electronic cigarettes introduced to Europe.

2008: Electronic cigarettes introduced to the U.S.

March 2008: Turkey's Health Ministry bans the sale and importation of e-cigarettes. Health Ministry Drugs and Pharmacy claims electronic cigarettes are just as harmful as regular cigarettes.

September 2008: The World Health Organization (WHO) proclaims that it does not consider the electronic cigarette to be a legitimate smoking cessation aid and demands that marketers immediately remove from their materials any suggestions that the WHO considers electronic cigarettes safe and effective.

October 2008: New Zealand conducts a detailed quantitative analysis and concludes that carcinogens and toxicants are present only below harmful levels. On the basis of the

findings, the e-cigarette is rated several orders of magnitude (100 to 1000 times) less dangerous than smoking tobacco cigarettes. The nicotine dose is comparable to that of a medicinal nicotine inhaler. Overall, the product tested was deemed a "safe alternative to smoking."
http://www.healthnz.co.nz/ecigarette.htm

January 2009: Australia bans the possession and sale of electronic cigarettes which contain nicotine, citing that "every form of nicotine except for replacement therapies and cigarettes are classified as a form of poison."

January 2009: Jordan's Ministry of Health bans the import of the electronic cigarettes, citing World Health Organization's health concerns. In a February 2012 review of the ban, the ministry claims that "e-cigarettes contain toxic chemicals that cause more health problems than the nicotine in normal cigarettes."

March 2009: FDA adds electronic cigarettes to Import Alert and directs the U.S. Customs and Border Protection to reject the entry of electronic cigarettes into the United States.

March 2009: Canada bans the sale, advertising and import of electronic cigarettes. Health Canada advises Canadians not to purchase or use them, claiming they contain a "known irritant" (propylene glycol.)

March 2009: Hong Kong Department of Health bans electronic cigarettes. The maximum penalty for possessing or selling e-cigarettes is a HK**$100,000** fine and two years' imprisonment. Since smoke-free tobacco is prohibited in Hong Kong, the ban on e-cigarettes continues to leave high-risk cigarettes as the only legal tobacco product available.

March 2009: FDA notifies electronic cigarette company "Smoking Everywhere" that its shipments have been refused entry into the U.S. The FDA maintains that electronic cigarettes "appears to be a combination drug-device product" that requires preapproval, registration and listing with the FDA.

May 2009: Action on Smoking and Health (ASH) files a petition to the FDA, calling for FDA regulation of electronic cigarettes.

April 2009: Smoking Everywhere (renamed as Tobacco Vapor Electronic Cigarette Association, **TVECA**) files a federal complaint seeking an injunction against the FDA with respect to the FDA's attempts to ban the import of Electronic Cigarettes. Smoking Everywhere contends that the FDA has no authority over electronic cigarettes, as they are a "tobacco product" and the FDA's attempt to regulate them infringes on Congress's intent to withhold FDA jurisdiction over tobacco products. They contend that electronic cigarettes are not "drugs," "drug delivery systems," or "drug device combinations."

May 2009: **NJOY (Sottera)** joins Smoking Everywhere lawsuit against FDA.

May 2009: The Electronic Cigarette Association (ECA), now closed, is formed. They were a trade association made up of electronic cigarette producers, distributors and retailers; whose aim is to speak on behalf of the electronic cigarette industry, especially in response to health concerns, and to help institute industry standards.

May 2009: FDA tests 2 brands of electronic cigarettes, NJOY & Smoking Everywhere. 18 cartridges are tested.

Tests reveal trace amounts of tobacco-specific nitrosamines (TSNAs) in the liquid in levels comparable to those found in FDA-approved nicotine cessation products. The liquid of one cartridge is found to contain a non-toxic amount (approximately 1%) diethylene glycol. TSNAs nor diethylene glycol is detected in the vapor. Some cartridges labeled as 0mg nicotine are shown to contain trace amounts of nicotine.

June 2009: President Obama signs into law the Family Smoking Prevention and Tobacco Control Act 18, giving **the FDA the power to regulate the tobacco industry**. Although nicotine and cigarettes as a whole cannot be banned outright, flavoring such as fruit or mint can. Additionally, new tobacco products seeking to enter the market will be required to meet FDA pre-market standards, which could affect electronic cigarette regulation.

June 2009: Panama bans the importation, distribution and sale of electronic cigarettes.

July 2009: FDA files a supplemental brief in the Smoking Everywhere lawsuit referencing the Family Smoking Prevention and Tobacco Control Act. The FDA contends that it still has authority over electronic cigarettes and FDA stand behind the decision to label it a drug-device combination. "FDA found, after examining the product, the claims made in the product labeling, and information SE submitted to FDA, that SE's product met the definition of both a drug and device under the FDCA." http://www.fda.gov/

July 2009: Two months after testing, the FDA issues a press release discouraging the use of electronic cigarettes and repeating previously stated concerns that electronic cigarettes may be marketed to young people, lack appropriate health warnings and that they contain carcinogens and toxic chemicals such as diethylene glycol, an ingredient used in antifreeze. The FDA did not reveal that the carcinogens found were similar to those found at the same levels in FDA-approved nicotine cessation products, nor that the amount of diethylene glycol found would not be toxic. The FDA also did not disclose that neither substance was found in the actual vapor to which the user is exposed.

July 2009: FDA's May 2009 study is reviewed by scientific consulting firm Exponent, Inc., in a report commissioned by NJOY. Some of the criticisms of the FDA study, as set forth in Exponent's report, are poor standards of documentation and analysis and failure to perform relevant comparisons to FDA-approved nicotine replacement therapy products, which Exponent claims contain TSNA levels comparable to those of electronic cigarettes. The study concludes that the FDA's claims of potential adverse health effects were not supported by the study. http://www.njoythefreedom.com/

July 2009: Israeli Health Ministry bans e-cigarette sales and importation.

August 2009: In a Washington Times op-ed, Dr. Elizabeth Whelan, president of the American Council on Science and Health, calls the FDA press statement about electronic cigarettes "***distorted, incomplete and misleading***" and meant to "scare Americans" to stay "away from these newfangled, untested cigarette substitutes -- better to stick with the real ones."
http://www.washingtontimes.com/news/2009/aug/06/fda-smoke-screen-on-e-cigarettes/

August 2009: The State of Oregon files two settlements that prevent two national travel store chains, Pilot Travel Centers and TA Operating, from selling NJOY electronic cigarettes.

In addition, the company must give the Attorney General advance notice that they intend to sell electronic cigarettes in Oregon, provide copies of all electronic cigarette advertising, and provide copies of the scientific studies they maintain substantiates their claims. **NJOY voluntarily stops all sales in Oregon**.
http://www.doj.state.or.us/releases/2009/rel073009.shtml

August 2009: Oregon Attorney General John Kroger files a lawsuit against Smoking Everywhere, alleging that the Florida-based "electronic cigarette" company made false health claims about its nicotine delivery device and targeted children with sweet flavors. Smoking everywhere refuses to settle.

August 2009: Brazil bans the sale, importation and advertisement of electronic cigarettes.

August 2009: **Suffolk County, NY** passes first legislation banning indoor use of electronic cigarette in areas where smoking is also prohibited and bans sales to minors.

August 2009: Saudi Arabia bans sales of electronic cigarettes based on the statement made by the US Food and Drug Administration which had said [e-cigarettes] "contain harmful carcinogenic and toxic substances, notably diethylene glycol, a toxic chemical used in antifreeze."

September 2009: California passes a bill to ban the sales of electronic cigarettes in the state. Governor Schwarzenegger *vetoes the bill* stating, "If adults want to purchase and consume these products with an understanding of the associated health risks, they should be able to do so unless and until federal law changes the legal status of these tobacco products."

October 2009: Consumer Advocates for Smoke-free Alternatives Association (CASAA) forms and board members elected. The organization is made up of both consumers and retailers, with the mission to ensure the availability of effective, affordable and reduced harm alternatives to smoking by increasing public awareness and education; to encourage the testing and development of products to achieve acceptable safety standards and reasonable regulation; and to promote the benefits of reduced harm alternatives. In order to ensure CASAA is first and foremost a consumer-based organization, the number of vendors elected to the board is limited so that consumer board members control a super majority.

October 2009: UK ASH recognizes that products should be made available that deliver nicotine in a safe way, without the harmful components found in tobacco, but those attempting to quit should use conventional NRTs. http://www.ash.org.uk/files/documents/ASH_715.pdf

October 2009: Amazon.com prohibits sale of electronic tobacco products on its website.

October 2009: **PayPal freezes accounts of electronic cigarette vendors in the U.S**. and prohibits them from using the service; however, vendors outside of the U.S. are allowed to continue using PayPal for electronic cigarette sales.

December 2009: New Jersey State legislators pass a bill including electronic cigarettes in the state's public smoking ban.

December 2009: NJOY announces it is discontinuing, in the U.S., the availability of all flavors except its traditional tobacco flavor and menthol. The move aligns the flavors offered by NJOY with those allowed for combustible tobacco cigarettes under the Family Smoking Prevention and Tobacco Control Act.

> January 2010: Judge Leon grants the injunction sought by Smoking Everywhere/Sottera **prohibiting the FDA from seizing e-cigarettes** as drug or drug/device combinations.

March 2010: The American Association of Public Health Physicians submits two Citizen Petitions to the FDA, one asking for reclassification of e-cigarettes to 'tobacco product' and the other asking for a follow up statement to the July 2009 press conference.

March 2010: First Vapefest™ is held in Richmond, VA

March 2010: Ministry of Public Health bans the import and sale of electronic cigarettes in Thailand. It warns "the cigarettes contained more nicotine than normal ones."

April 2010: The American Academy of Pediatrics, American Cancer Action Network, American Heart Association (AHA), American Lung Association (ALA), American Legacy Foundation, American Medical Association (AMA), Campaign for Tobacco-Free Kids, and Public Citizen file a motion requesting to support of the FDA.

April 2010: CASAA assists the Midwest Vapers Group in persuading Illinois legislators not to pass a law which would prevent convenience stores, tobacco shops and mall kiosks from selling e-cigarettes.

June 2010: American Medical Association (AMA) House of Delegates (HOD) passes a policy urging the FDA to regulate e-cigarettes as **drug delivery devices**.

July 2010: Singapore bans e-cigarette importation, distribution and sales. Fine is of up to $5,000 upon conviction.

July 2010: Marine Corps Base in Quantico bans e-cigarette use in its facilities.

August 2010: CASAA joins other e-cigarette and reduced-harm smokeless alternative proponents in filing a brief in the Sottera vs. FDA case. Others named on the brief include The American Council on Science and Health, National Vapers Club, and Midwest Vapers Group.

August 2010: Oregon's Attorney General John Kroger reaches a settlement **preventing** the two national travel store chains from selling e-cigarettes.

August 2010: Air Force surgeon general's office last week categorizes e-cigarettes as "tobacco products" and prohibits their use in most Air Force facilities.

October 2010: First VapeFest™ is held in UK

December 2010: U.S. Court of Appeals in Washington rules the FDA can only regulate e-cigarettes as a **tobacco product**, unless therapeutic claims are made.

February 2011: Study is published in the American Journal of Preventive Medicine reporting that electronic cigarettes are a promising tool to help smokers quit, producing six-month abstinence rates that are better than those for traditional nicotine replacement products.

http://www.ajpm-online.net/webfiles/images/journals/amepre/AMEPRE3013.pdf

February 2011: The **U.S. Department of Transportation** says the **use of smokeless electronic cigarettes on airplanes is prohibited** and announces its *intention* to issue an official ban.

April 2011: FDA announces it will regulate e-cigarettes as it currently regulates traditional cigarettes and other tobacco products under the Food Drug and Cosmetics Act. However, any e-cigarette products advertising claims of helping the user to stop smoking or providing any other health benefit will be more strictly regulated as a drug or medical device.

April 2011: Tobacco Vapor Electronic Cigarette Association (TVECA) is formed, "an association of private sector companies engaged in electronic cigarette technologies." http://tveca.com/membership.php

May 2011: Argentina passes resolution banning the importation, distribution, commercialization and advertising of e-cigarettes and paraphernalia related to them.

June 2011: Venezuelan government bans use and marketing of electronic cigarettes.

June 2011: **First Vapestock™ held in Clearwater Beach, FL.**

August 2011: Study published in the journal "**Addiction**" provides *strong evidence that electronic cigarettes are being used with success by many smokers to quit smoking* or cut down substantially on the number of cigarettes they

consume, and that e-cigarettes are being used with success by many ex-smokers to remain off cigarettes.
http://onlinelibrary.wiley.com/doi/10.1111/j.1360-0443.2011.03505.x/abstract

September 2011: The Obama administration proposes banning the use of electronic cigarettes on airline flights, saying the "new rule would enhance passenger comfort and reduce any confusion." The Department of Transportation says that although it considers electronic cigarettes to be covered under the existing law banning smoking on airplanes, it intends to adopt a rule specifically banning them in the summer of 2012.

October 2011: The British Cabinet Office's Behavioral Insights Team (BIT) strongly endorses tobacco harm reduction in its first annual report. E-cigarettes are cited as potentially effective substitutes because of their behavioral attributes.
http://www.cabinetoffice.gov.uk/sites/default/files/resources/Behaviour-Change-Insight-Team-Annual-Update.pdf

October 2011: First VaperCon™ is held in Richmond, VA

October 2011: The results of the first clinical trial of electronic cigarettes, reported in the journal BMC Public Health, suggests e-cigarettes **may be more effective than traditional** NRT products for smoking cessation and may be particularly effective in smokers who are not motivated to quit. http://www.biomedcentral.com/1471-2458/11/786

November 2011: CASAA calls for members to urge the Alameda, CA City Council to remove e-cigarette use from a proposed smoking ordinance and arranges for locals to make public comments at the Council's first reading. **The** *ordinance passes* with e-cigarettes **successfully excluded**.

December 2011: Holland's Minister of Health, announces that the sale and import of electronic cigarettes is banned. E-cigarette sales will require a pharmaceutical license.

February 2012: CASAA successfully organizes local opposition to the Hawaii Senate Ways and Means Committee's proposed **70% electronic cigarette tax** in SB2233. The bill passes the ban on e-cigarettes sales to minors without the 70% sales tax.

March 2012: First VapeBash™ is held in Chicago, IL.

March 2012: United Tobacco Vapor Group Inc., a branch of the TVECA, wins a lawsuit challenging the Dutch Ministry of Health's ban on e-cigarette sales.

March 2012: Higher Court in Germany, instructs the state to **remove bans and warnings** about e-cigarettes. Court issues opinion that electronic cigarettes are tobacco products and not drugs.

March 2012: Consumer groups including CASAA, ECCA UK, Stelda NL (Netherlands), IGED (Germany) and ATACA (Australia) organize the first World Vaping Day, which takes place on **March 22nd**. http://www.world-vaping-day.com

March 2012: Nearly 200 of Germany's estimated 1.2 million electronic cigarette users march peacefully in Düsseldorf in protest.
http://www.youtube.com/watch?feature=player_embedded&v=4C0T2v0C4R8

April 2012: Venezuela's government threatens to punish with fines up to $8,400 for those who distribute or promote electronic cigarettes banned in the country for not having permits or corresponding health records.

Since then there has been consistent and ongoing changes and events that continue to this day:

Sites you should know:

www.CASAA.org

www.SFATA.org

www.TVECA.com

www.ACSH.org

For more information contact:

www.VapeMentors.com

support@VapeMentors.com or call 949-495-6162

stay in touch for information on our new books:

"Masters of Vape"   ETA, Q1 2015

"Vape Freedom Tour"   ETA Q3 2015

www.ingramcontent.com/pod-product-compliance
Lightning Source LLC
Chambersburg PA
CBHW051723170526
45167CB00002B/774